KU-651-391

# Everyday Heaven

## Journeys Beyond the Stereotypes of Autism

*Donna Williams*

Jessica Kingsley Publishers
London and Philadelphia

First published in the United Kingdom in 2004
This edition published in 2010
by Jessica Kingsley Publishers
116 Pentonville Road
London N1 9JB, UK
and
400 Market Street, Suite 400
Philadelphia, PA 19106, USA

*www.jkp.com*

Copyright © Donna Williams 2004 and 2010
Printed digitally since 2010

The right of Donna Williams to be identified as author of this work has been asserted by
her in accordance with the Copyright, Designs and Patents Act 1988.

All rights reserved. No part of this publication may be reproduced in any material form
(including photocopying or storing it in any medium by electronic means and whether
or not transiently or incidentally to some other use of this publication) without the
written permission of the copyright owner except in accordance with the provisions of
the Copyright, Designs and Patents Act 1988 or under the terms of a licence issued by
the Copyright Licensing Agency Ltd, Saffron House, 6–10 Kirby Street, London
EC1N 8TS. Applications for the copyright owner's written permission to reproduce
any part of this publication should be addressed to the publisher.

Warning: The doing of an unauthorised act in relation to a copyright work may result in
both a civil claim for damages and criminal prosecution.

| Blackpool Borough Council | |
| --- | --- |
| 3 4114 01804 387 6 | |
| Askews & Holts | 01-Apr-2016 |
| B WIL | £15.99 |
| PAL | |

Library of Congress Cataloging in Publication Data
A CIP catalog record for this book is available from the Library of Congress

British Library Cataloguing in Publication Data
A CIP catalogue record for this book is available from the British Library

ISBN 978 1 84310 211 3

To my inspirations, Sheila, Bobeth, Serge and, of course, my wonderful husband Chris. And to
the holistic doctors and clinicians who have dared to be pioneers in the labyrinth of autism and
think outside of the box. Finally, to Jackie Paper, Margo, Monty and Jean. Always with me.

# Foreword

Autism is a fruit salad and every journey with it is different. There are questions of where does condition end and self begin or are the two so intertwined as to be interchangeable. There are questions of culture verses cure or treatment. Where is that ethical, spiritually healthy, socially humane? There are questions of whether there is autism or autisms, whether autism makes one alien amidst general social or, like looking through a microscope at humanness itself, does it illuminate experiences we all have, uncover things people hide about their own world and the secrets of self just under the surface or buried deeply.

I was assessed as psychotic at the age of two in a three day inpatient hospital assessment in 1965. By late childhood I was still echolalic, had a language of my own, was labelled disturbed and still being tested for deafness. My meaning deafness was discovered when I was nine and interventions led to me gradually acquiring and becoming fluent in 'functional speech' but it would be decades more before I could use that to deeply express and gain answers about my own 'fruit salad' or the passions, fears, perspectives I had about others, life and myself.

Living with meaning deafness, meaning blindness, disconnectedness with my body, mood, anxiety and compulsive disorders and gut, immune, metabolic disorders as part of my own fruit salad, my dance with autism has been a lively one, a dynamic one. As one of the most well known people diagnosed with autism in the world, it has been a controversial journey. I've captured that journey across nine books in which *Everyday Heaven* is book four in my four stand-alone autobiographical works.

The first one, Nobody Nowhere became an international best seller in 1992 and is now set to become a Hollywood film. Against one of the challenging social backdrops, I wrote of my simultaneous battle to join the world and to keep the world out and the adaptations and magic in between those battles. The book became a touchstone in the autism world but, more importantly, illuminated the human condition itself.

*Somebody Somewhere* followed a few years later, again becoming an international best seller. In it, I became a qualified teacher meeting children and adults with autism and began teaching others about the my world, how to 'Simply Be' and the exploration of self versus condition.

By the mid nineties my autobiographies had a worldwide following. I followed the first two with a third book, *Like Colour To The Blind*. Here I explored the inability to tell compulsion from want, to read one's own emotions and body messages, discovered what a visually fragmented face, a body, a world can look like through tinted glasses and journeyed into the world of Augmented and Facilitated Communication.

*Everyday Heaven* is perhaps the most laugh-out-loud of the four autobiographical works, which is strange for it's a story of beginnings and endings, of transition and emergence, of life and of death. It is a story of spirituality and development and what happens when your life has become a stagnant pond and you transform it into a flowing brook.

On some levels it is one of the first published autobiographies about autistic marriage and soon enough about divorce but also a book about an autistic perspective on death and loss.

Laced with humor throughout, Everyday Heaven navigates the reader from a veneer or contentment into the turmoil of death, separation and divorce. But as endings close one door, others open and the book soon springs into a coming-of-age story about the sudden clumsy, funny but beautiful emergence and exploration of sexuality and orientation. It is also story about health and facing the stark realities of being someone with primary immune deficiencies facing my own death in my mid thirties. And it is a book of hope and how treatment turned that around and simultaneously set me free from Exposure Anxiety's labyrinth of involuntary avoidance, diversion and retaliation responses.

Along the way, I became not only an author and a teacher but an international public speaker, an autism consultant who has worked with hundreds of people with autism. I became a partner, a friend, a fool, a pioneer, a candle to others and a controversy. As I moved from autism to artism, I became an accomplished painter, a sculptor, a singer-songwriter and screenwriter. Most recently I became a band manager of Donna and The Aspinauts and wrote, produced, directed and performed in rock musicals.

I can't say I managed all of these things through the defeat of my autism because in so many ways it was my autism itself which gave birth to all of these things. The once meaning deaf girl became the singer and musician. The once meaning blind girl learned to see through her hands, became proficient in gestural signing and a sculptor. The person once crippled by Exposure Anxiety learned that typing could set her free and became a writer. The person who had danced with mood, anxiety and compulsive disorders since the age of two learned to seize life where she could, never waste it. The person who had battled to feel her body, own it, love it and fight for it, became a performer who would touch the lives of others though using it. The warrior who had battled life, selfhood and autism until she learned that loving achieves more than fighting, took that lesson forth as a lecturer, teacher and consultant. I hope you enjoy Everyday Heaven as a stand-alone adventure in my autobiographical series.

# Everyday Heaven

'I think you will always be a travelling girl,' said Fritz, the German man in the seat next to me, in his broken English. He was quiet, gentle and jolly. I had only known this man for the thirty minutes I had been the hitchhiker in his car as my music played on the radio, my voice filling the void while the world whisked by. That's the way dreams work, I guess. Already, though, I sensed a strong spirituality about him as though, like me, he looked not just past the image of the person, maybe even beyond time and space. The wildness in me had found his words and the faraway look familiar when he had said it, and I dreamed that in me came a thought-feeling: no, Fritz, you got it wrong.

The daylight of dawn at its peak kissed my eyelids and woke my soul on this crisp blue-skied September day in Wales. I opened my non-registering eyes and they stared blankly ahead into a meaningless array of colours and patterns that happened, by chance, to be the bedroom wall and the window looking out onto the fields of our Welsh farm. I loved those dreams of my music, dreaming I was hearing it played on the radio. But it was never real.

Behind me was Ian, tall, willowy and sullen, who wouldn't be awake for a few more hours. It had only been seven months ago that I had bought this big patch of green in the middle of Welsh-speaking nowhere land. This was Ian's dream of the ultimate privacy away from 'the world'. Still like brother and sister after ten months together, he'd been ready to leave my cosy one-bedroom shoebox by the train station in Essex after becoming a predictable piece of the furniture there. Either he was going alone to get himself a flat somewhere, or I would buy a farm. And not just any farm. He had a prescription for his ills, his progressively paranoid aversion to what we called 'the world'. It had to be a farm away from all other neighbours, enclosed, if possible, within its own land; and of course the brand new Mercedes. Essentially, Ian had ordered a modern-day castle, complete with golden carriage. So, not wanting to shake up the security I had now established in living with this 'best friend', I bought his dream and we moved from my rusty Ford Escort and tiny miner's cottage to be peas rattling about in this pot and shopping in the Merc. And I held keys to neither. I would forget them if I was entrusted with them. Like the money and the phone, it was much more sensible that Ian handled them.

The once-in-a-lifetime book royalties had covered the costs and the place was massive as requested, with three upstairs bedrooms, one for him, one for me, one for us. Downstairs lived a massive kitchen, a dining room, a sitting room, a lounge room. Then outside, the stables with several outbuildings – and there were only two of us and not so much as a cat or its fleas to share it with. All that mattered was that I had a friend and was not alone.

It was only ten months before that Ian had helped us find out that we each wanted to be married.

'Checking' operates on a preconscious level. It is a way of tapping into the sensing reality and avoiding interpretive thinking which blocks out awareness of things it assumes are not 'us'. Asking oneself a question can't evoke a purely emotional response because it addresses the mind, not the emotions. Making a provocative statement out loud before a witness, however, stirs up a sense of sudden exposure at the statement, evoking either a non-response if the statement is untrue or one of 'caught me' if the statement has some truth in it.

We took it in turns stating, 'I want to be married'. When the response was evoked, it came with no thought, no understanding of its context. It worked on a distinctly separate system from thought or reason.

We never considered the fact that although we'd checked about whether we each wished to be married, we hadn't checked on Ian's part about why he wished to be married, nor on mine about who I wished to be married to.

Ian's statement evoked excitement. Mine left me beaming like a child caught with my hand in the sweet jar, and the more I wished it off my face, the more the expression insisted on breaking through to show itself to the world. In the next instant, a rather happy Ian determined his quite wealthy friend had to follow through with her wish to be married. There was only one problem. It was not him, but the Welshman, Shaun, I had always wished I'd been married to. But did I say anything? Did I defy his assumptions about my obvious want to be married? Did I fly in the face of his enthusiasm about my response and be open and honest that I was still in love with the Welshman, my once-upon-a-time love of my life, allergic to commitment? Nope. And here I was making the best of things with 'my friend'. I had broken rule number one, be honest with thyself and others, whatever the cost.

My head still on the pillow, my mind, now awake like a wound-up spring about to ping, was having intangible thoughts that evaded consciousness by just a step but were somehow still there like some waking dream. The expressive calling in me of unknown knowing drove my body away from the human toast next to me, out of bed, down the stairs and to the computer, grabbing my special tinted lenses and dressing gown left lying in my path to trigger me into taking it on the way. Can't do by oneself, for oneself, as oneself, but I was merely tidying the floor.

As I put my tinted glasses on, the bedroom sprang to life as more than colours and shapes now. The meaningless patterns and colours were now the window and the curtains and the view outside as my brain started now to keep up with the flood of what was coming in.

I had spent all my life struggling to voluntarily access and hold a conscious thought. I had loads of stored triggered ones like quiz show buttons which fired as if of their own volition whether fitting or not.

I felt alienated from the process of thought, and only consciously let in on the product, as though I was continually possessed yet able to consciously experience the possession after the fact. Through writing, all my unknown knowing typed itself out. It spoke to my conscious mind through my eyes as they read my words from the page. I had found a mechanism via which I could move preconscious unknown knowing into consciousness and it made me feel whole and in control of my life, my thinking and my expression.

Ian could help me use monitored conscious, accessed, self-expressive speech by setting up plastic cows through which I would play out who said what and went where and what the response was. But Puter didn't require spoken words. Puter linked directly from thought to fingers and back in through eyes to mind with no overload and no blah blah. Puter involved no weary physical mechanics of coordinating lungs and tongue and mouth and voice box and the conscious plod plod it took to retrieve self-expressive, non-stored words or phrases for speaking and shape them into a format that was easily comprehensible. Yet, Puter had no familiar smell and Ian did. Puter didn't do 'hair', running fingers through my long curls hypnotically till I felt inaudible purring. Puter didn't cook taste-buzz dinners or answer the phone, saying 'no' and 'she's not interested' on my behalf and stopping life from sweeping me away in an ocean of its wants in the absence of any awareness of my own.

'Er-er-ee-er-er,' said the computer as I started it up and started typing. 'Stop it!' I said to myself, as I remembered Ian's rule that was stored within the parent in me: 'No computer before breakfast.' And I needed a pee badly. And I was cold.

My body sat in the chair, my hands typing automatically, my eyes reading the unknown knowing that poured out from within me and greeted consciousness as the words hit the screen. If nothing else, I seemed always freed up to type. Pee, no. Get a jumper on, no. Get a drink or some breakfast, no.

The addiction to self-feedback in a world in which meaning still dropped in and out like faulty headphones, made it hard to move myself from the chair to fulfil what Ian and I had agreed was a sensible rule. The struggle between compulsion and want gripped my stomach and made breathing tight, forcing recognition. I got the message and with half of me still reaching for the keyboard, my body was on the way to the kitchen; breakfast THEN computer; I ordered myself about as Ian. Old dog learns new tricks.

It had taken me two days of good intentions diverted into everything from scrubbing the bathroom to cleaning out the chimney before I was finally able to get my hand and mouth in line with the phone, dial and get through to my younger brother. None of them had a direct address or phone number for me in case my mother got into one of her phases, so my contacting them was the only way to link up unless they left a message via my agent. My brother's voice was warm but self-protective and clear in spite of the ten thousand miles the sound had to travel.

'When you coming over here?' he asked.

'Soon,' I replied avoidantly.

'You got a date?' he questioned.

'Yeah, but not sure what it is,' I answered, knowing any information I gave would be siphoned out of him by my mother desperate for ownership and the social image it restored for her in the eyes of strangers, at the hands of guilt.

'You gonna see Ma?' he asked.

He knew the answer and he knew how I felt and why. He had been the kid sent to the front door to get me from my flat when she insisted on keeping control. If I couldn't see her, he was not allowed to stay and talk to me. Still, here in our adulthood it was as if the role had not changed. Still, being her confidant these days it was impossible he could fail to be loyal and ask.

'No,' I answered.

I dreamed of change like any such child does. Wake up one day to find the horrors are gone, that the brittle sharp-edged ball of barbed wire has become a place of rationality, equality and calm in which it is safe to be oneself. But here in the now, the reality gripped my body with a sickening dread.

'She's changed, you know,' said Tom referring to her drinking and violence now replaced more harmlessly with poker machines and bingo. 'She's mellowed out.'

But nothing could sell me on the idea. Her feelings for me as nemesis, owned object and confidante, back-to-back with the abuse she'd never publicly admit, didn't have to be my baggage to carry, even if she was my mother. If she had changed, good luck to her, and I would truly celebrate such freedom from my safe distance knowing that she'd have changed for her own good and that was for her to own. But you can't change what you've never owned up to, so there was no hope. In any case I needed no open invitation for a place in this ongoing soap with its emotional and psychological rollercoaster. Even if inspired by others to change, ultimately nobody changes for anybody else but themselves, and if they claim to, then it's probably temporary suppression rather than real change or development. If the junkie gets clean, you don't test them out by presenting them with drugs. I felt that mentally and emotionally, to her, whether she'd ever admit it or not, I was those drugs.

The plane landed in the tiny Asian island of Bali on the way. Ian held my sweaty hand to save me buzzing or floating off into AWOL as we shuffled our way through the sweaty crowd of airport chaos, collecting luggage, showing papers here and there, exchanging monies and being shuffled further along towards the door.

Outside of the door, the thick hot humid air wrapped me in, heavy against my skin. 'Taxi, you want taxi?' came the voices of short, dark, smiling men clad alternately in colourful sarongs and shorts with American sneakers.

We bundled into a taxi and rumbled down potholed roads, packed tightly up against our luggage, sucking in hot air in stifling, unairconditioned discomfort. Ian looked at me through his tinted lenses with wide boggledee eyes, and I looked back at him through mine as the taxi trundled us off into the unknown. We were heading to Ubud, by the monkey forest. It was two hours away.

The roads were lined with palm trees and wildly colourful plants. Brightly dressed people walked along the streets carrying baskets on their heads. Cane-woven baskets and bamboo cages lined the streets filled with chickens, fish, nuts and fruit. Emaciated stray dogs and cats sat or lay looking loyal on the front doorsteps of bamboo houses or ran out suddenly into traffic every so often. By sharp contrast, well-built clay villas with their intricately carved wooden doors had on their doorsteps well-fed pets, which looked like a whole other species.

At the monkey forest, trees towered high over us like earth-bound demi-gods. Monkeys of all sizes hung from the trees like Christmas decorations. On the ground, they flocked among the tourists, grabbing bags of peanuts to help themselves rather than wait for the charity of human beings.

Ian, who found human company so difficult to manage, loved the company of animals and had brought some nuts to feed them. A large monkey had walked boldly up to him and grabbed them like a bully, walking off with them without the slightest hint of gratitude and with no intention or desire to share the booty.

Ian went swimming in the sea, and as his mirror, I followed, submerged in turquoise-blue water, surrounded by bright colourful fish and swimming over coral cities and waving anemones. I saw a shark, big and gray, and grabbed Ian's attention under the water and signed to him 'Look!'

Unlike me, Ian had not only visual perceptual problems, but also eyesight problems. Being shortsighted and without his prescription glasses, Ian took my wild gesticulations to mean there was something worth exploring and swam straight for the direction of the big, gray shark.

I froze in the water, waiting to see him torn apart in a bloody mess before my eyes. Instead, the shark swam away and Ian swam back, with a flippant expression that said, 'Well, I looked, but there wasn't anything there!'

The plane arrived in Australia and we made our way out of the air-conditioned, artificial atmosphere of the airport. We stood in the early summer air of Terra Australis in shorts and T-shirts and sandals as it poured down with heavy, cold rain and a sharp wind bit into us. Ian looked at me, and, as his mirror, I looked back with the same fleeting and desperate look. Then as him I ran back into the warmth of the airport to unpack and get changed. He grabbed clothes, I grabbed clothes. He went to put them on, I went to put mine on. We re-emerged dressed in warm winter clothes, got into a taxi and went to collect our hired mobile home before heading off to see a wise, and witty, old owl friend called Theo Marek.

I hadn't seen Theo Marek or his family for a long time. Back then, now six years ago, our sessions were about things like the definition of 'friend' and the meaning of 'social' and how to attempt eye contact more regularly than once every twenty minutes.

The Mareks were away and we were invited to make ourselves at home in their house. We parked the mobile home out the front and went inside. After looking around, we unpacked our things and slept on the sofa bed like a pair of cats, weary from a long journey.

I had known Bryn now for eight years but hadn't seen him for five years. Bryn, now newly diagnosed with Asperger Syndrome, was the first other person 'like me' I'd ever met, and meeting him had both knocked me flying and found me at the same time. Though I hadn't been able to directly express or share this belonging at the time, since writing my first book, I'd tracked Bryn down to tell him I now had a word to describe why he was 'like me'. He had seen Theo Marek, as I had, and, at the age of forty, had been given a word to make sense of forty years of pain and misunderstanding and abuse at the hands of psychiatry.

I had come to mean the world to Bryn, and he would never understand if I had visited Australia and not seen him. Ian had me check for a want, to be sure the idea to see him wasn't out of compliance. The want was there. I had wanted this contact, wanted it in my own right and I felt shamed for it. I told Ian I had to see Bryn to measure the changes in my feelings since having seen him last. That was the logical truth, but the logical truth is only ever half of the story. The emotional truth was that it was also just some warmth that was in me that found the castle walls too cold no matter how close Ian and I were in our symbiosis.

Due to leave the next morning, I phoned Bryn with the shock that I was here. With Ian, I had gone through our system of 'checking' and found that what he could tolerate was twenty minutes. If Bryn could make it to the Mareks' house in twenty minutes, I would see him, but he could only stay twenty minutes. It never occurred to me I could dare tell Ian to just take a bloody walk or something, or that I could have seen him on his own.

Bryn arrived, the highly intelligent and equally simple tall, gentle-giant teddy on legs that I remembered. He sat down on a chair on one side of the room and seemed like a flower planted out in a desert. I sat on the sofa, and Ian sat next to me as if staking his territory. It was painful. It looked like an interrogation. Bryn fumbled as he tried to make connections, and his aloneness was tangible. I felt Ian withdraw, glass walls going up. The energy in the room was like the tapping upon brittle glass, and it was all my fault. This was my need. If I didn't have it, Ian would not be in such pain. If I had not existed, Bryn would not have liked me so much and would have had no need to see me. If I had not existed, I would not have had the want. I tumbled inwards, but my imaginary friends, Willie and Carol, were not there to rescue me. Dissected and thrown into the rubbish with Ian's assistance in order to prove he had no feelings, there was no stuffed little Travel Dog to turn to. Sold to the antique shop with Ian's assistance, there was no Orsi Bear. I had left my own world behind in joining the world, and as I now turned inwards my own world was like an empty shoebox.

Without any external sign, without words or looking at me, without body language, Ian withdrew into himself; and within me a sense of abandonment resonated as surely as if he had played a chord and I was the instrument. Without conscious intention or choice, and without any overt message, instinct had me respond, by closing Bryn out. Ian thawed. We were speaking a silent dialogue in a world without words or sign. My fluffy edges were doing me a disservice. I was simply too sensitive.

I sensed Bryn's exclusion too and looked at him in an unexpressed 'sorry'. In me was a sharing that couldn't get out in spoken words or actions. It was as though invisible threads had tied us all into straitjackets. The spoken words between us all were like the irrelevant and deceptive surface ripples of a violent undercurrent. The formality of it was stifling and needless, yet my deep empathy for Ian had me adhere to it as my own creation.

Bryn had stayed the allocated twenty minutes, and I looked to Ian with the hope the castle walls could take the strain. His face gave nothing. I could not slap his insecurity in the face. I could not wound the wounded. I could not smash the mirror. I was a hypocrite, bad at living my best advice. When it came to the tough love I so advocated, I was hopelessly, sickeningly, co-dependent.

Bryn got up to go. He put out his hand to shake hands with his now married friend. Ian looked at me to confirm whether I had a want to do so or not. I managed to shake hands, the feel of Bryn's big rough hand leaving a slow-to-be-processed touch-print on mine, and I felt no compulsion to erase the deed, to disassemble it. It was welcome there. I felt the rattle of prison doors.

Surely, in the slow blink of a preoccupied eye, my way out of my inner prison, my door to freedom, couldn't have led to an external prison with Ian as warder? How could I feel trapped by the man I cared for and who seemed so clearly to care for me? I needed to get this damned self-protective aversion to my own existence to leave me alone so I could jump up and save my own arse.

We were on the road again. The closer the signs got to the little town of Broughton, the harder I found it to breathe.

Unable to get ongoing paid employment, my younger brother Tom had lived with his girlfriend and my mother until about a year ago. He now lived away from her, together with his girlfriend on a dusty golden farm with crisp, crunchy straw grass and clay thud-thud earth in the middle of nowhere on the outskirts of this two-horse town.

He didn't know we were coming. I hadn't been able to trust that he wouldn't tell my mother. And if she'd known, in her inability to tolerate any loss of control, there'd have been no way she'd have respected my desire to stay away from her. Even if it would have cost me seeing my brother, I couldn't play the game and cared nothing for her public advertising as just a mother who loved her estranged daughter, always so worried about me, about my mental state. The reality could never be wished away nor, to stay safe, should it have been.

What if my mother was there with him? What if he wasn't home? What if he was glad to see me and I wasn't glad to see him? What if it was around the other way? The emotional impulse fired with each intangible half-thought and the lack of connections gave no answer, no reply, so the dread merely built in the absence of resolution or imagination.

We got to the gate, opened it and drove along the long driveway to the farmhouse. 'If my mother's there, we're driving away,' I informed Ian. 'It's OK,' replied Ian, 'your brother doesn't know me, I'll just get out and ask if she's there and if she is, I'll get back in the van and we'll drive away.'

Ian got out of the car and walked up to the house. A young easy-going man came out in well-worn cut-off denim shorts and a head scarf, together with a pretty young woman dressed in flowing white seventies 'hippy' clothes. Ian spoke to him and signalled to me that it was OK. I got out of the car.

Tom was overwhelmed and shocked and clearly very glad to see me. He looked at me with his freckled face and laughing green Chinaman eyes and shook his head, looked at me again and shook his head again. He looked as if Santa Claus had arrived. He just kept smiling and saying out loud to himself and the world, 'It's my sister. I can't believe it's my sister come to visit me.'

Tom's girlfriend approached me, her fluffy, long hair tied up in a knot on her head and wisping around her freckled Australian face in all directions. They'd been together for just over five years and I'd never met her.

'Hi, I'm Sandy,' she said, looking from me to Tom and back again.

'I'm Ian,' said Ian with as much presence as can be in such an asocial and quiet man. Then we went up the steps and into the farmhouse.

The house was full of their artwork, beautiful colour contrasts and shapes, harmonious ebb and flow of colour and pattern. Tom's, by contrast to Sandy's, abstract and impressionistic in a way which spoke of the sensory, non-interpretative, alien world where pattern is seen first and meaning second.

In the corner was the guitar I had bought Tom as a surprise because I'd felt he had the blues and so needed one. He told us how he played it for the birds who would all come down to him from the infinite country sky and gather to listen.

Outside, Tom, Ian and I climbed up onto the seven-foot-high concrete water tank. 'I come up here and sing,' said Tom, putting his head into the hole at the top and making some noise before finally adding, 'Its got really good echo.' When Tom's head came out, I mirrored him, easily swapping loyalties to put mine into the cool dark space, and made some noises too. We went to climb down. Tom jumped off the side. He was twenty-four and he still seemed to think he was Superman.

Tom's eyes, as always, were squinted up tightly against the biting sunlight. It had always, been so for him, since he was a baby and then a toddler. As I watched him, they now flitted from place to place as he spoke or listened, his attention haphazardly drawn to a series of unconnected, seemingly irrelevant points of focus at a pace that made him appear edgy. The anxiety of the child was now the shaking of the man, and his hands trembled as mine had until I'd changed my diet to avoid food allergies, dairy and gluten intolerance and to address the vitamin–mineral imbalances I had been diagnosed with.

Since having my lenses, I was curious now watching Tom. I asked him about how he saw. He explained that he saw in the finest detail, far more than most people. He explained how he saw the patterns of things and every component of the whole. Though the colour and shade of my lenses was different from Ian's and that of other autistic and dyslexic people who had them, I was curious how mine might affect Tom. I took them off and asked him to try them. His forehead uncrumpled and his eyes stopped squinting. He looked around in a flowing connected line, his eyes no longer flitting seemingly indiscriminately among things that jumped into his attention. His body relaxed. 'You should see about trying out some of these,' I told him. 'I think they might help you.'

It had been five years since I had seen him and I had only been there for the agreed twenty minutes, and now it was time to go. Ian, who never saw me close to anybody else or free to share in a 'my world' way, seemed uncomfortable. Though he sat patient and tolerant and put no pressure upon me, I could rawly sense his self-exclusion and, without seeing it, could feel his aloneness and abandonment.

I felt the lead weight of guilt and I felt pressured by this delicately triggered intense empathy I had for Ian's obvious sense of abandonment – this sense of other so strong that it sweeps away the grip of self.

'We've got to go,' I told Tom.

'Oh no. Do you have to?' Tom replied, disappointed. Without even looking at Ian, I knew.

'Yes,' I replied.

'I love you, sis,' Tom said, looking at me. I avoided his eyes.

'Why?' I asked.

'I've loved you ever since you shoved a pillow up into my coat and sent me flying headfirst down the stairs on my back,' Tom added, his eyes dancing with a wild smile of happy remembrance of a belonging that I wished so much I could have had back.

As we drove away, Tom was still saying 'I can't believe it, that's my sister'. In my mind, I now knew, it was possible for me to live as myself in his company as his sister, and I knew that even if I didn't know if I loved him, I certainly liked that person who was my brother, and that was, at least, a very good place to start.

As we drove down the road, the dust flew up at the windows enveloping us in a cloud and I felt like the prisoner who'd been let out for a visit and was now trundling back to prison.

I looked at Ian. He wasn't forcing me to do anything. He was on my side. He was my special person in this world. He would never hurt me or stop me from doing anything I wanted. He cared about me. And yet, I had no sharing in me right now for Ian and could only think of me and Tom and Tom and me and Tom and himself.

I felt emotionally constipated, as though I had tears in me that had turned to cement and couldn't come out. The feelings drove thoughts like the sticks to the drowning man. Reasons to turn back flooded my mind as grounds for bargaining with guilt and with the warder within me that would have me be loyal to our insular relationship in which we'd vowed not to let other people into our lives on the understanding this would keep us 'safe' – safety in a vacuum.

About a mile down this road, the physical distance between Tom and me ticking by on the odometer, I finally grabbed one of the sticks.

'Can we go back?' I asked sheepishly, guilt gripping my voice box. 'There is something I have to give Tom.'

'Are you sure?' asked Ian, careful to make sure I wasn't acting out of fear or compliance. The right answer was, 'Forget about it', 'No, you're right, I don't really want to', 'I changed my mind', but the answer that peeped out in a whisper was 'Yes, I'm sure.'

Ian drove back down the dusty clay road and through the gates and down the drive. Tom and his girlfriend were sitting outside the farmhouse, surrounded by golden fields with the sun shining down hard.

Tom stood up as the mobile home approached. He was shaking and had been crying.

'It's all been a bit much for him,' his girlfriend said gently.

'I can't believe it,' said Tom, 'two visits from my sister in one day. I can't believe it.'

'We came back to give you these,' I said, handing him my spare pair of tinted lenses and remembering to include Ian in my statement.

Though the colour that would work best for him would probably not be the same as mine, they had seemed to do him at least some good, and he didn't have the money or social resources to get some for himself. Tom took them, looked at me and put them on. I looked at my brother.

'We're really going now,' I told him. Before we parted company, I took his wrist and held his hand up in front of me. I put my own hand up to meet it and we did 'mirror hands'.

I was nervous now. Though he promised he'd say nothing, by now Tom would have told my father, Jackie Paper, that I was here.

Like Tom, I hadn't seen Jackie Paper for five years, and I had stopped calling him or writing to him too. It had been a year since I got the news from my agent that he had gone to hospital, diagnosed with cancer. It had been no shock. I'd heard the word when I was nine or ten; the phrase still stuck in my head in the tone in which it was spoken, obsessively, over and over, in celebratory tones: 'Look at him, he's losing weight, you know he's bleeding from the arse now. He's been to the doctor's. It won't be long. The cunt's got cancer.' But that was then, neatly filed away under 'Well, we all moved on and survived. We're all still standing'. My agent had told me my father had had an emergency operation and was on chemotherapy. I behaved as if this was new news. The only thing that said it wasn't was a poem, written years ago, about a girl stirring gravy which went onto her father's plate. A poem I never dared send. A poem only I could bear to see. After all, I was 'crazy' back then, wasn't I? Nobody would believe someone who had been 'crazy'.

I wrote to him then, knowing his terror of hospitals and doctors and needles and death, and told him not to fear the Reaper and that death, if he had to face it, was just a journey he hadn't been on yet. I had been able to do so according to the rules of Exposure Anxiety; can't do it for myself, by myself, or as myself. I had convinced myself I was doing this for him.

I had written to him in case I didn't get to see him again, but I had written to him to set things straight so that he knew who he was to me and who he was not. He was Jackie Paper, a valued person, a comedian, a megalomaniac, a womanizer, a manic-depressive, a dyslexic and crazy man who tried to be everybody's pal and who happened to be my biological father.

Being five years old in an adult body, he hadn't been able to be a father in the supportive sense of the word, but in his own half-arsed ways I always felt that the crumbs he threw were gold. As long as we both knew the reality, nobody was being conned or confused and all was as it was meant to be with nothing missing.

Wanting to outrun the passing on of messages and the potential of my mother heading me off, Ian drove the half an hour straight for Jackie Paper's country house where he lived with his girlfriend.

Through the town and out into dirt roads and golden fields again, Ian pulled up outside his house and parked the mobile home.

My stomach full of rocks, I looked cautiously at the house, waiting for someone to come out. Nobody did. We walked up to the house as though it would suddenly say 'boo' and I tapped on the sliding glass double doors, my feet stuck firmly to their place but my soul tearing at my body with the message 'Run', 'Get away'.

There was nobody home and a stored phrase from some film came to mind: 'temporary reprieve'. Analytically and externally, I regarded this phrase. So, I was the prisoner on death row. What, though, was the fear?

'He's not home,' I said with an absence of disappointment, as fear handed my voice box back into the hands of my logical self. Inside, my chemistry screamed for control over my body and the burning emotional urge to run and run and run was like the call of addiction. My movements flitted with my internal wildness bound and gagged by the intention of my mind that stood firm, committed and unswayed in knowing I was here to see my father. At least diet had given me this much control, though this chemistry still plagued me badly.

'What do you want to do?' asked Ian. That was the red flag to the bull and my chemistry wrestled with my tongue. I bit the bastard and got control. 'Stay,' I replied, slamming the door on the escape hatch, for though fear had its own 'wants', and 'wanted' them with a vengeance, I had developed a strong sense of who I was and what I wanted beyond the compulsive and impulsive dictates of fear. Fear would also call itself 'self' and, given the chance, rule my life with my name as though its defensive manoeuvres, its rules, hiding techniques and war strategies passed for true intention and self-expression, but it no longer had me fooled.

A car turned into the street and drove towards us in a cloud of dust. It was, unmistakably, Jackie Paper. A cross between Robin Williams, Gene Wilder and Spike Milligan, Jackie Paper got out of the car and walked towards us with his stilted, boppy, salesman walk. His eyes, squinty, like Tom's, half laughing and half closed against the sunshine.

'Miss Polly,' he said in his warm and husky, though controlled, voice. My self was running inwards. I couldn't turn outwards. It made me want to scream and attack. I kept the lid down.

'This is Ian,' I said, deflecting the sharp sense of other that was impinging upon me.

'Glad to meet ya, mate,' said Jackie Paper in stored salesman style, extending an automatic quiz show hand like a pop-up boom-gate at a children's school crossing.

Ian visibly withdrew at the unintentional confrontation, his hands pulling backwards out of the way.

'I don't like to shake hands,' he choked in a half-strangled whisper.

'No worries, mate,' said Jackie Paper, turning a page and heading us towards the house with his girlfriend clucking in raspy blah blah noises like a stressed-out half-strangled chicken which fell meaning-deaf upon my overloaded ears, shut down in the grip of Exposure Anxiety.

We entered the kitchen, and Jackie Paper flitted like a manic puppy, making himself, the retired man with cancer, appear tremendously busy and desperately in need. Inside of me, I wanted to tell him that I knew his fear, his shame, his feelings of redundancy, the rawness of self-exposure, particularly at a time when his various operations and chemotherapy had robbed him of his dignity. I wanted to tell him to 'Simply Be'. I wanted to tell him I understood what was in him because I took after him, and in this sense who he was who was within me. I wanted to tell him I could see he was totally out of control but knew who his real self was. I wanted to tell him a lot of things, but I couldn't say a thing. Instead I sat there imprisoned like a puppet with a 'yes' string and a 'no' string as his girlfriend made 'conversation' and my living skeleton father, Jackie Paper, made endless strings of phone calls and put on postures of the big man taking charge.

I walked to the end of the lounge room. There were photos of his girlfriend's children and their sports trophies among the gaudy ornaments my sensory buzz-junkie father had brought home like a human bowerbird. Cat statues, a musical silk flower arrangement under a glass bubble, a lamp that lit up when you tapped it, another lamp full of fibre-optics that lit up in different colours, a clock with plastic mock-gold sequins and red and black velvet sat awaiting guests. On the dresser, standing propped like in a bookstore, were my bound and published books, my photo jumping out from each cover, simultaneously the trophy and the photo of one of his three children, and the only one represented in this house.

There was an air of disgust in Ian and it blew over my own unprocessed feelings like a wind that tainted them. I had felt deep sadness for my father's aloneness, that his children, that I, had not even cared enough, been a daughter enough, to have sent him real photos, that instead he had displayed my books in their place. I had felt intense guilt that this had put him among a world of millions of fans, yet he was my father and I had accorded him little more recognition than I accorded them in compliantly responding to their letters, along their tracks, never mine. I felt sorrow for what was missing and that there would never be time and space within his currently lived lifetime to fill it in. I felt raw self-exposure caused by feelings and the realization that my father, in displaying these books, was expressing a felt closeness to me as his daughter, a closeness I felt unworthy of in not being able to openly acknowledge it or reflect it back.

I also felt guilt in the presence of Ian, estranged from his own father, at being someone whose father clearly and unashamedly had known me and felt something for me and that, mingled with the spices of fear and anger that are part and parcel of the recipe of dysfunctional families, I too felt something for him. I looked at Ian and compulsively reflected back at him what it seemed he would feel most comfortable to hear. I reflected a mutual but unfelt disgust. Whilst Ian had disgust at what he perceived to be my father's gaudy display of his daughter's fame, I felt only disgust at myself and a rebelling against the intensity of felt emotion that would make me vulnerable and exposed, but I allowed Ian to believe what he needed to believe.

Jackie Paper broke away from his business-business and came towards us with stiff but animated doll-like movements, referring enthusiastically to the books.

'I've told everyone about your books,' he said beaming. 'Everybody's buying them.'

And unlike Ian, I could hear no self-backpatting in his voice. He had not promoted himself in doing this. He had felt pride, intense pride. My father was proud of his daughter. I sensed Ian's distaste. I turned inwards and said nothing, gave no acknowledgement. My father's words, like a ball thrown, bounced back emptily as though they'd bounced off a wall, and I hated myself for it.

In the twenty minutes we'd been there, Ian's unexpressed discomfort was a lead weight that I sensed brutally.

'We have to go,' I said in the words of a human puppet as if to the wind.

'You just got here,' said Jackie Paper. 'Can I get you something? I'll make you a cup of tea.'

Guilt and shame rose in me and no tears came. I was undeserving of them.

'No, we really have to go,' I said, mechanically.

I could have killed myself right there and then and still felt unworthy of such a reprieve. Why could I not assert my own existence in the presence of someone to whom I could relegate the responsibility for my own existence? Damn the many faces of Exposure Anxiety. Damn the lure of its traps, the easy path of expressive non-existence.

Jackie Paper walked us out.

'Nice meeting you, mate,' he said to Ian with the utter genuineness of the five-year-old inside this dying man of fifty-eight.

Ian, quiet, gentle and turned inwards, accepted the remark but said nothing in reply.

'It was nice to see you Miss Polly,' he said to me, his voice rustic and warm.

'See ya, Jackie Paper,' I said through the opened window of the car door from the passenger seat as Ian started up the mobile home.

I knew it was the last time I would ever see my father and after not seeing him for five years, we'd only stayed twenty minutes. I was a hypocrite. Here was I hailed internationally as the woman brave enough to face her emotions and express herself as herself, to share and to reach out, and here I sat, a sell-out to myself and to my father, the man I took after. As we drove away I felt the door to my invisible prison slam.

My instinctual and defensive fear of emotion and of self was on its way down the road of self-denial. It had my voicebox now. It had my tongue. Yet I still had my feelings and my thoughts. Even if this Exposure Anxiety cut me off from getting a grip on expression through my body, at least I knew my own truth. As I sat my inner self and my outer appearance split in an internal war, and the scenery flashed by as Jackie Paper moved out of the now in space and time. And now, buried alive, I didn't feel at all comradely with Ian, the man I'd sold out for. I felt angry and resentful and unfree.

Ian and I pulled into the last in a string of caravan parks. The birds warbled with the wild sounds of the Australian bush. The rustle of dried, papery gum trees and their smell of eucalyptus made me feel wrapped up and home. Ian seemed at home here, at ease, falling in love with the place, yet I couldn't tell him I felt home, couldn't dare the sell-out that he might feel in hearing that this foreign place, ten thousand miles from where we lived, was home to me. Chains, chaining chains.

We went walking, looking at birds and sharing the smells and the sounds of crackling leaves and the intricate structure of flowers.

Theo and Judy Marek arrived at the beachside caravan park to meet us. I had family feelings for these well-adjusted people, and they had them for me too.

Ian cooked dinner for the four of us. Judy, her usual warm and friendly self, stayed with him in the mobile home, perhaps not even sensing his discomfort at what felt like an unwelcomed invasion. However friendly and real she'd been with him, he'd found no comfort in it, no rapport, no warmth and couldn't help but feel she'd 'checked him out' with the inaudible cluck of a mother hen watching out for her chick: me.

Theo Marek came outside with me and in the absence of Ian we talked out loud to ourselves of change and fathers and whatever fluff topics came up. He was a solid and real person, and I felt sure in his company, not at all floundering, as our feet kept a rhythm on the sand and held the interference of Exposure Anxiety at bay.

After dinner we all went out walking, picking up shells and sticks and rocks and sharing patterns.

The four weeks passed quickly, and Ian had fallen in love with Australia and its odd plants and smells and sounds and animals. We had one last person to meet, my elder brother, James whom I'd found too sharp-edged, too formal, too defensive, too quick and had feared all my life.

I had always felt rushed and never ready for his flippant quips which always came, never able to keep up. In my literal simplicity, I would take his words too personally or find them confusing, his movements too sudden, unpredictable and startling. The only self-expressive speaking I had risked with him had been the one or two phone calls I'd made in the last year, and I still had never spoken to him face to face as myself.

There was no backing out. I had seen the others so it was only fair I saw James. I put in my coins and the phone rang sixty miles away. James answered.

'Do you want to meet?' I asked him.

'Just tell me where,' he replied.

We arranged to meet in the middle of nowhere and told each other what vehicles we'd be in. Ian and I cooked lunch in the mobile home while we waited the hour it would take for James to drive to where we were.

His car was there and his sunburned scruffy freckled face beamed at us under a mess of sundried wisps of early-balding hair like yellow-gold cotton candy. I was struck by the realness of my brother, the self-confessed dinosaur. Born an adult, he'd never been a child, and here, my elder brother by sixteen months, aged just thirty-two, was a well-worn tyre.

'Hiya, mate,' he said in his 'everybody's pal' salesman tone. 'So good to see ya.'

This was the brother who'd hated my guts and for whom the feeling had been entirely mutual. I smiled too and peeped as much of a mousey 'hello' as my selfhood could get out through the guarded gates of self expression.

'You must be Ian,' he went on sticking out his hand like a cowboy in a Western. 'Good to meet ya mate.'

Ian stood there, defenceless in his gentleness and his indifference, with nothing to say and no want to share or know this man.

'Sorry,' said Ian, 'I don't like to touch people.'

'No worries,' said James seeming not at all put out. 'Hey, you're married to my sister. Guess that makes you my brother-in-law.'

We drove to a site we'd picked out, James following us down the dusty park track. He got out of his car and joined us in the back of the mobile home.

At first he just stood, rather limp like a rag doll with his head tilted a little and a boyish tentative look on his face that might have been puzzlement. Then he moved across the room in chunky solid steps, threw his arms wide and engulfed me in them, squeezing me tightly. I was still processing his steps across the room by the time he had hugged me and was just starting to process the hug by the time it was over. I stood there stunned, not quite sure what he'd got out of that or why he'd done it. Though as toddlers he'd been my 'friend' until he realized I was oblivious to him, as children and adults we'd always been either strangers or enemies.

James sat down again, beaming and clearly happy. It was a connected happy and I couldn't understand it.

'I have so much to tell ya,' he said. 'I've realized so much.'

We walked among rows of roses and Ian and I stroked the velvet of the roses and breathed them in. Without words, I called James over and signed for him to smell a rose.

'Take time out to smell the roses,' I said to him, reeling off a learned line in my own voice.

We all sat among the roses, and James talked for two hours. I listened as best I could, reminding him to slow down for me and for him, as he repeated himself like a scratched record, each time thinking he'd said things for the first time.

'I'm sorry I'm going on and on,' he said, 'but I have to get it all out. I've been wanting to say these things for about five years, but there's no-one else I think would understand them. I tried to write them but I just get a few words out and it all gets jumbled up and doesn't make any sense.'

He was silent for a while and shook his head as if saying something to himself.

'Hey, how's that,' he said out loud, 'all my life I've been looking for someone who can really understand me and, what do ya know, it winds up being my crazy sister.'

James had defied the twenty-minute curfew and had been with us for three hours. It was time for us to go. In all that time, Ian had spoken only a handful of sentences. Though he had liked my brother, if he'd had his choice it would either have been just him and me or just him, which sometimes amounted to one and the same thing.

'Well, mate, what can ya say?' said James, looking like a child standing at the door at the end of a good birthday party.

This rough and ready man who had once been my tormentor, now stood looking as happy, coy, exposed and vulnerable as a four-year-old.

'It's been good to see ya, mate, really good to see ya,' he went on, getting into his car.

'Seeya, Ian,' he called, giving a parting wave from the car window.

As James drove away, it was as though the five torn pieces of paper were no longer scattered to the wind, irretrievable. Though I still found it unsafe to see or speak to my mother, and James and Tom were still estranged from and embarrassed by my child-like father, and though it inevitably wouldn't last, we no longer seemed to be some drawn and quartered entity of biologically related strangers.

Across ten thousand miles of earth, we had arrived back to the winter of a Welsh December. It was our third Christmas together.

Whatever Christmas was for other people, I had always had my own version. As a teenager, I had gone into the city with sweets and given them to homeless people on the steps of the train station just like the men in Santa suits had gone around giving them to shoppers in the days leading up to Christmas. Later, I'd delivered home-made mini 'Christmas trees' to people's front doors, decorating a branch with sweet wrappers I had found and tin foil and leaving it on the doorstep. Other times I would fill up empty bottles with pine needles floating in water, decorating the bottle with tinsel to produce 'Christmas in a bottle', and leave them for people to find.

Christmas with Ian had been different. He was allergic to birthdays and Christmas. We had had a 'Simply Be' Christmas Picnic once, one of those freefall experiences, uncontrolled, wild, free and self-owning, but that was as far as it went. Ian, though, was starting to outgrow this aversion, but although he was well trained in Xmas hoo ha, he didn't know how to 'do Christmas' spontaneously as himself from feelings.

We decided to go and buy Santa outfits. We phoned around and found somewhere and went and bought them. With Ian as Santa and me as Mrs Christmas, we headed off for the toy store.

Ian looked away while I looked around and found some things I thought he might like. I took them to the counter and put my finger to my lips, signalling the shop assistant to say nothing. She took my money and wrapped the things in store paper and bags. Then it was Ian's turn.

As we walked through the streets, children looked and old people smiled. I felt exposed and lemony, my hand around the throat of fear. Ian walked along feeling vulnerable, dressed up as Santa in tinted glasses but with none of the warm feelings to go with it he looked the grimmest Santa I had ever seen.

We got home and dished up dinner and then got the presents out and unwrapped them. Ian looked upset with himself. Christmas was a pair of shoes his utterly logical and practical mind would probably never fit.

It was a cold wet January with ice on the ground, and the farmer's sheep were having early lambs. One by one there would be complications with a pregnant sheep rolling onto its back and unable to right itself, and there were many times we had caught them just in time and turned them over. An orphaned lamb stood on the bloated upturned belly of its dead mother out in the field and bleated with no reply.

Pregnant sheep were brought into the stables to have their lambs in relative warmth. We watched newborn lambs take their first steps and watched the mother sheep get to know them and them get to know life.

A mother sheep had three lambs. One stood with raspy breathing on little stick-legs with saggy old-man wrinkles of fine dirty-white woolly velvet. Another stood staring at the wall, its rib cage rising and falling.

'Would you like a lamb?' asked the farmer. Ian and I looked at each other. Our wants broke through in smiles driven by big feelings. Ian chose the one staring at the wall.

The mother sheep had bad udders and couldn't feed them all. There would only be enough milk for one to survive. No sooner had we accepted one than we were offered another. We chose the one that seemed least involved with the mother. Both, as it turned out, were girls.

We grabbed straw and plastic and headed into the house. They would live upstairs in the tiny little box-room next to the bedroom. We laid the plastic and the straw and went for the lambs.

Ian carried one and I carried the other. Like little sacks of bones in our arms, they were tiny, not more than one foot from nose to tail with saggy skin and short felt-like greyish wool. They bleated as we carried them, a warm flat sound, not at all like the harrowing wail of a human baby. The mother called back from a distance and they continued calling. It was a sad but happy moment when two sides of life collided.

Long after the door to the house was closed, the lambs continued to call out into the nothingness. We answered them in sheep with 'maaaaa'. Eventually, they started to answer each other's cries, exploring each other's bodies, prodding each other's tiny, bony, fragile bodies in search of a teat and, at various times, suckling brutally on each other's fleshy armpits.

Ian filled up the bottles with milk made from powdered sheep's milk and we made our way back up the stairs to the box-room; it was ironic that I could feed the lambs but spend the whole day trying to get on track to feed myself.

'What will we call them?' Ian wondered. 'What's French for sheep?'

'Brebis,' I replied. 'What's German for sheep?' he continued.

'Schaf,' I replied. And those became their names: Brebis and Schaf.

We stood at the doorway watching them over a partition we'd put up to keep them in. They were covered in each other's excrement where they'd been exploring one another's smells and body parts, and were now curled up together, exhausted and shitty, tucked into a corner of the bottom shelf of the bookcase in the little room full of straw. It was one of the most beautiful things I ever saw. Ian and I looked at each other like parents cooing over our new twins.

Ian had no desire to have children, and I had no desire to have children to Ian. He couldn't stand their noise and smells and would exit a train carriage to get away from them. I found children interesting, thought of them as wonderful living art and often caught them looking at me as though they knew I was pretty much three or four or five underneath that adult skin. I cared about them and had empathy with them in their struggles, but the idea of being responsible for them filled me with dread. I was barely able to stand being responsible for myself. I always thought I'd be the sort of mother who would lock herself in the cupboard or run away if a child was too demanding or clingy. The sensory hypersensitivity, emotional extremes, muddle-headedness and the involuntary aversion, diversion and retaliation responses of Exposure Anxiety were certainly nothing I felt privileged to pass on; and if a child had the same difficulties I had, it would be condemned to a life in a dietary wheelchair. So pretty much, it was agreed we both didn't want children – me reluctantly, Ian gladly. Yet here we were with these two babies who came to follow us everywhere and cried relentlessly for company and bottles and, with no mother sheep to snuggle up to, had to have their trembling little bodies wrapped up with home-made knitted coats each day. Somehow, the fact they were so mono, so all self, no other, so caught up in their own worlds, meant they didn't trigger the fight-flight responses in me which were so highly programmed to sense the slightest social invasion.

They went to the toilet everywhere, and we were surprised they didn't go when we were holding them. Schaf was gentle and simple in her ways, and it showed in her eyes and her pleasantly smiling face. She liked to snuggle and was otherwise not too fussed with learning about the world. She had taken to Ian and would climb up on him like a small dog and go to sleep. Brebis was wide-eyed and twitchy with a serious look. If ever there was a sheep with Attention Deficit Disorder, she was one. She was ever curious, a bag of beans prancing in the snow and kicking her heels, who didn't seem to have much time for just resting or snuggling up. Nevertheless, she took to me and followed me everywhere like Mary's little lamb.

Together, Ian and I fed them four times a day from morning till late at night, and I found the routine easy, doing for them rather than for myself. We chased them around with remote-control cars, letting them explore these strange moving creatures. We brought them all sorts of things to smell and chew and feel and carried them high up in the air, showing them the world from all the perspectives they hadn't yet seen and took them running in the snow. In turn, they were alert and more clever than most sheep. They would play hide and seek with us like little dogs, chasing us around the perimeter of the house and waiting for us to come after them. They developed games among themselves, running along routine pathways as fast as they could and turning sharp corners with wild, uncoordinated (and hilarious) little sideways goat kicks in mid air. Brebis came to play a game in which she would head-butt the ball to me. They developed a language between themselves, able to signal each other in sound and stance when something worth being involved in had suddenly shown up. It was no longer just Ian and me. It was Ian and me and the lamblets.

The lambs progressively outgrew the room and then outgrew the little shed we'd moved them out to. They were approaching sheep puberty and chased us around the outside of the house, maa-ing desperately until we came out, then round and round the outside of the house again, springing and clicking their hoofs in the air before racing each other playfully down an incline into the open-fronted garage. I swear they were laughing.

As they began to seriously head-butt the back door, I helped Ian to build them a wooden house. Then a few bald rose bushes later they were moved out into a field we fenced off for them. Their house was a chalet-style wooden house with a door, skylights and two Perspex windows they could look out of. It faced our own house directly, and every night they would call for us as we left their field for our own house. We would see them standing in the doorway and sometimes watching us through their windows. The lambs had taken Ian's focus off me, brought us together and had instilled a sense of belonging and family to the farm.

It had been six weeks, and after a week of being on my hands and knees nibbling grass, the lambs were now eating grass too and the bottles got less and less till they were gone. Each week the lamblets got chunkier and woollier. They would still come running over with happy leaps and kicks under the increasing weight of evolving sheep fat. They got rounder and rounder and bigger and scarier as they hurtled towards me with a girth of two feet wide and growing.

We had taken them to meet other sheep, the farmer's sheep and lambs in the other field. They didn't like the idea at all and stuck close by us, away from those foreign creatures. It was clear that these sheep-lambs identified themselves as human, and because we spoke to them in their own sheep sounds they never really seemed too confused about who or what we were. We were 'like them'.

A publicity tour was coming up. We were going to Norway in March to promote my second book, *Somebody Somewhere*. It was hard to leave the sheep-lambs. We weaned ourselves off them and them off us, watching them from behind the curtains as they watched the house for the slightest sign that we were coming out to be with them. A day here, two days there, sometimes we couldn't stand it. Schaf would stand there staring at the house, bleating till she was hoarse. Ian's feelings went out to her.

'If I don't go out and see her, she'll hurt herself,' he reasoned.

'If you do go out, then next time she'll do it twice as badly,' I replied.

We said 'maaaa' to them as we left and they replied. We were on our way to the ice and snow of Norway.

We had been filmed by a Norwegian TV company, a programme filmed weeks before in Wales, but appearing on the TV in Norway the week we arrived. We visited a field full of ancient wooden cottages, wore ice grippers strapped on to our shoes as we walked down streets thick with ice reflecting light between the gray clouds above and were captivated by architecture and symmetry. Walking down the street, a woman grabbed Ian by the arm, jabbering at him in Norwegian. Ian pulled away and the woman fussed about, sorry for her over-excitement. I had simply been glad it hadn't been me. Back at the hotel, we got into the elevator. A woman grabbed the door and climbed in, lunging towards me in excited tones as she rambled on about having seen me on TV. I had been interviewed now over eighty times in countries all around the world and got fan mail every week, but an author is usually not visually known. This was the first time I'd had to deal with this sort of confrontation. We felt glad we were going back to Britain where I was relatively unknown.

'Would you come back to Norway some time?' asked the publisher. 'Maybe you could give a talk here.'

Ian stood expressionless.

'Maybe,' I replied.

'When's the next trip?' asked Ian with a tone of dread once we were back at the hotel room. There would be other publicity tours to handle when I got back home. There was a London talk in a few weeks and then two American conferences I had agreed to appear at in April. Then there was a Japanese documentary two months after that in June.

'That's it for this year,' said Ian with a hint of desperation. 'Don't take on any more.'

'OK,' I replied.

But we had hardly been back at our farm long when the post, inevitably, brought in more requests. Would we do a Canadian documentary filmed here in August? There was also a request to do another American conference in September. That would make three American trips for the year. Ian agreed that in the absence of a 'not want', we'd do these things. We checked, and because Ian had no distinct 'not-want' in him, it was agreed we'd still go.

'But no more,' said Ian. As much as his mind insisted he'd had enough, something in him still wanted in, or perhaps that something in him just couldn't stand to feel left behind if it had to see me go it alone.

April was here already, and the date for my talks in Connecticut and Syracuse were on the agenda. People had been after me to do talks for four years now and I had always refused. These were my first conference talks, and in spite of all the talking I had done through my books, it was others who had been out there giving such talks for years and I'd just started. I wanted to see if I could do it and I wanted to see what it held for me.

We arrived in America and were staying in a Connecticut doll's house with wallpaper patterns that jumped out into your face and coordinating quilt covers.

The tap in the kitchen spun around in every direction. I played with it and it buckled somehow, leaving everything grossly out of alignment, like something Dali might have used for a surrealist sculpture. It was hugely degoitzian (over-stimulating) and it tickled me intensely, each tickle, unprocessed, topping the last, until I was flooded, wild, laughing and crying and unable to breathe.

The emotion in this manic oblivion ran so high it was getting painful and my ears voomed with sudden rushes of blood as adrenaline escalated. I turned my back on the monstrosity, hoping that would stop it from affecting me. The tease of what I would see when I turned around just sent me higher. I was way off planet earth now. Ian stood there ordering me out of the room like some German officer. I threw a tea towel over the monstrosity, to make it disappear and held my stomach, now cramped from wild laughter.

'Out, out!' said Ian, ordering me next door.

I slid to the floor, propped against the wall, waiting for the tickles to die down so I could breathe.

The next day was the conference, and a limo arrived to take us there past an array of dolls' houses till it gave way to a big building. I had needed the toilet for over an hour but Ian had shown no indication of needing to go.

'Do you need the toilet?' I had asked.

'No,' Ian had replied.

And so, I was stuck.

The shuffling of hundreds of people slowly quietened in the auditorium. Ian had had a bottle of water, and although I was dying for a drink I more desperately needed the toilet. Nevertheless, I had to take the drink whilst Exposure Anxiety would let me. Ian drank, I drank. I had almost made it to the toilet door as we passed it after drinking the bottle of water. No, came the retaliation. No time. I felt rage. I had been waiting now for what seemed all day. If only Ian had needed the toilet. I had been announced. Now I was most certainly unable to use the toilet. Suddenly, Exposure Anxiety shifted. Now I could go to the toilet, I needed to go and I should go. To hell with the crowd waiting, my name having been announced. I turned around and ran back to the toilets.

'We don't have time,' urged Ian putting out a hand.

I complied and headed through the doors to take my place as a speaker.

Through the doors, Ian and I went up the stage steps and sat on the wooden stage. Ian clipped on my microphone and I looked up at the ocean of friendly faces. Then I burst into tears and cried for a few minutes as the audience sat in polite quietness.

I wiped my face and slowly began to read my pages. Slowly the meaning fell into the meaningless words on the page and I looked up at the faces, testing the water, seeing if I could handle acknowledgement of them and expression of me so confrontationally.

This was a conference put on especially for me to speak, and all these people were here to see me and I was talking for them. There was warmth and kindness in their faces. Their eyes seemed to be reaching out. I swayed between the inclusion being offered and the escape route offered by fear of connection. This was a social ocean and I was bobbing in the tide. Someone was crying in the third row. I worried that I had hurt her feelings. A woman in the front row made excited noises and jumped up from her seat, lunging straight for me and doing involuntary tic-like boggledee-boo with her hands in front of my face in a private autistic language.

I finished speaking. The audience had already been asked not to applaud. The effect of heightening the already unbearable level of Exposure Anxiety I was feeling would have made applause about the worst punishment a crowd of people could have inflicted. As my words stopped and the silence thickened, the whole room stood in awesome and respectful silence. I was so touched at the consideration I had lived without most of my life, consideration from a room of hundreds of people, that I cried as I walked down the aisle created by this wall of human bodies. The woman, once terrified of being herself and being touched as herself, of compliments, of direct and personal expression, now walked straight through the ranks of the forgiven enemy.

Out of the doors, my body erupted as tidal waves hit. The adrenaline of Exposure Anxiety and general information overload was running up at danger levels. My ears roared with the rushing voom of blood pumped furiously around my body by a cocktail of adrenaline and other haywire body chemistry. The tremors had hit like a junkie going through withdrawal, and every nerve end screamed in a wild physical chaos as panic noises began to emit from my half-strangulated voice-box now held in the tight grip created by overload.

Tic-like, my hand flicked wildly by my side and I began to jump, trying like a demon possessed to get the wildness of the adrenaline high out of me. Ian held my hands and helped me jump on the spot. In such intense physical discomfort, it was even then still clear why I did the things that caused the Exposure Anxiety and emotional overload that brought all this on. Just to think of it warmed me up inside, wrapping me in a security no other human being could give me. I was kicking fear smack in the face and showing it whose life this was. I was a dog biting back its own fleas.

My enemy had taken twenty-five years of my life, and it thrilled me to have it by the neck. It could attack my body with the wild rush of intolerable chemistry but I was in control of that body and the life lived by it. It was fear that would drive me to hurt this body. I fought fear to love it and care for it. It was fear that tore at every fibre with the wildness and the tremors in this state of adrenaline addiction. It was me who gave my body a rhythm to comfort it and then held it when it had calmed. Finally, the adrenaline rush abated. Exposure Anxiety on hold, I seized the opportunity to take a long-awaited pee.

The next stop was Syracuse in the state of New York. I would do it all again. It was part of my personal private rehab programme and my road to freedom. If I could kick Exposure Anxiety in this way, I could conquer it in all its lesser evils. I would conquer it from the top down.

The plane landed, and a hairy man and a hippy woman greeted us and whisked us away into the night and into the woods.

On arriving at the house in the woods, Ian was depressed. His depression made me anxious. I didn't want him to have trouble. Mostly, I didn't like the defensive, controlling, authoritarian and distant him he became when he had trouble, when he'd lose all processing for relative and personal significance and plunge into Aspergerian little-picture literality and 'logic'.

With the best of intentions, the house was a sensory catastrophe. It had been closed up for months and was like a second-hand goods shop, cluttered with every imaginable piece of clutter.

Our escorts had come in with us and were still waiting to get to know me. I had hardly spoken. I picked up a cushion and it slimed in my hands. Its insides were so silky that the cushion felt like it was full of goo. That was it. Already raging with adrenaline looking for a place to express itself, I launched into a sudden manic outburst. The tickles had got me in an instant and topped themselves several times in thirty seconds until their once reasonable-looking guest looked like some wild thing from a cartoon. I was out of control, tickled wildly and inescapably from inside until I was crying and coughing and laughing, one after the other like a one-man band.

I rid myself of the cushion in a mighty fling outside of the double glass doors like it was some kitchen frying pan that had caught fire. I sat trying to calm myself, the tickles in me addictively seeking to still top themselves. It was hard work to fight this addiction to my own chemistry.

'Sorry,' I said eventually, regretting I hadn't spoken to these people sooner, so they'd at least have seen the human being in me first and not second.

I felt compelled to solve Ian's discomfort and woke up early and piled all the degoitzian, sensorily full-on (boggledee-boo) into one spare room and closed the door. I scrubbed the thick chunky green-gray mould from the shower curtain and took the crusty scalies off the bathroom basin. I aired out the rooms and unpacked some of our things. By the time Ian got up, it was a new house.

Ian went outside, surveying his surroundings. We were by a lake. He decided to make a raft. I walked about collecting sticks and hitting them into the air. Then I went inside, watching the talkies quacking on the TV: flick, blah-blah-blah, flick, blah-blah-blah, flick. I watched Ian through the window as he built his raft and took it sailing out on the water held by a piece of string, sending it out and drawing it back whenever it went too far.

A warm, softly spoken, hairy American arrived to take us for the three-hour trip to Niagara Falls.

Wild aqua torrents danced in a symphony of movement as they roared and splashed their way downstream and over the edge of a huge horseshoe. White seagulls hovered in the air over the edge where the water fell to the depths way, way below. It was hauntingly beautiful and eerie. I'd seen this before as a young child in a repeated dream when I was about three, looking down into the aqua blue that went down and down and down. I felt like jumping. The old call to fly got me, and an adrenaline rush began to call me, beckoning me with the promise of a high. I could fly, fly like the seagulls, just over that edge, just like in the movies. Who was Donna Williams anyway? Since disclosing and leaving behind my two imaginary friends, I no longer used the strategy of attributing my actions to these other somebodies and the constant distraction of Exposure Anxiety was on my back night and day. For the sake of flying off the edge of a cliff into a moment of perfect aqua blue, I'd have given up all I had fought for. But I didn't want to distress my host; and besides, I had promised Ian I would try not to indulge the wildness too much, not buzz too high.

B ack on the Welsh farm Niagara Falls was now just a memory. The page of May had come to an end and the entire month of June was dedicated to a Japanese documentary team who'd be with us for a whole month. We would have a day off every few days, and the calendar was marked up in chunky black felt-tip pen with 'Japanese' and 'us'.

I had been approached a number of times to do documentaries and TV spots. The ideas and frameworks for them seemed so entirely foreign and outside-in. Finally, though, I had realized that not only could I set out the format for interviews, there was no reason why I couldn't set out the entire format for a documentary. In response to a request to do a documentary, I put it to them that I would if it was done by my structure and totally within my control, if it could be from an inside-out approach. They agreed.

The Japanese crew drove up the long driveway of our farm in a big van and climbed out. We had met two of them already, the director, a waif-like woman with a wispy voice who spoke very little English and the coordinator, a firm but eager-to-please diplomat who was Japanese but spoke good English. Both of them were nervous and it was clear from the feel to them that they saw me as 'little Donna' who was unpredictable and a mystery. With them was a small Japanese cameraman with the staccato pace of a little terrier dog, and a stocky dark-haired freelance Irish technician named Mick, who stood at the doorstep somehow naked in his realness by comparison with the others.

The crew entered the house with the camera rolling, pretending we were meeting them for the first time when we had already met at least two of them twice. It seemed silly and pretentious, as though they expected me to play along with a lie or as though they felt comfortable distorting reality. It was not a good way to start off. With reality, you knew where you stood and you could trust your own memory, your own values, your own mind. With bullshit, you could be swept along to anywhere and nobody was reliable. Without understanding why people bullshitted and without being able to read the cues, you could never tell where reality ended and bullshit began, so you couldn't trust.

'We know who you are,' I interrupted, cheekily making it clear I wasn't a co-conspirator in the bullshit.

The crew entered the house, so many people all at once all focused so intently upon me, so directly and so personally. Ian felt bombarded and had a monkey-arse grimace plastered on his face, his mouth pulled tightly into a mock smile and his eyes not smiling at all.

The people had brought a present, a tradition in Japanese culture. It was a book of Japanese characters. It felt wrong, terribly wrong, to be confronted like this and given something so directly by people we hadn't even decided we liked. It was as though these people were trying to guarantee feelings they hadn't yet earned. There was so much pressure from them that it felt invasive and overwhelming, like the unwelcome but intimate attention of a stranger who makes uninvited assumptions of closeness and acts upon them. There is a difference between 'friendly' and 'friends'.

The coordinator and the director exuded a truckload of emotion and gratitude in whiny, apologetic, emotional tones, like people tip-toeing over glass.

The short little cameraman whipped around like a Wild West cowboy, his camera balanced on his shoulder as he ran about shooting us with utter recklessness. Mick held his big hands still and calm, half biting his lip with the look of empathy one might have expected from an animal lover visiting a circus full of performing animals. I took in this silent dialogue and showed no recognition of it as the remaining members of the crew, in spite of good intentions, unwittingly established a strong sense of this being the scene of 'the Donna Williams Zoo'.

I had lost my grip on meaning and had gone off for a wander into the lounge room where I caught myself playing with my familiar friend, the light switch, and waited for everyone to disappear. After they all left, I wrote them a long letter.

The next day, they arrived to find a closed door with a sign on it telling them to turn off the cameras and informing them that to arrive with the cameras rolling was intrusive and bombarding and that it showed no respect. From inside of the house, Ian and I watched their van pull up and saw them get out of the van, as expected, with the camera rolling. From behind the curtains, we watched the eager non-English-speaking cameraman walk briskly up to the sign on the door and film it. Mick, who'd understood the words on the sign, signalled to him to put the camera down. Once they'd disarmed themselves, we finally opened the door. I walked up to the coordinator and handed her my note, telling her I'd meet them in our caravan near the house. Then I walked inside again closing the door.

The letter read:

*To the Crew,*

*Yesterday, the interviewer, coordinator, cameraman and the technician arrived at our front door filming us without considering what our capabilities were. They came in assuming the roles typical to introduction and gift giving. This was alien, imposing, and even though the intentions were good, the actions felt loaded with assumptions and expectations. From my side, it could never have created the sense of warmth or familiarity it was intended for. It created instead a sharp sense of intrusion and alienation. All of it was done in their time and in their ways, and it created such an overwhelming tidal wave of other that I could only seek to hold onto my selfhood by shutting them out. Ian was less lucky and was swept up into the selfless portrayal of the pleased-to-see-you role they clearly expected; a role that gives the sought-after outward appearance of so-called 'normality' in spite of having no connection to what he said and did. What the crew failed to consider was that we were not left with any processing time or space to find out what any of our own wants or likes may have been. Upon reflection, we'd have told you you must enter our sanctuary on our terms or not at all because it was you who asked the privilege to enter our world. We already choose where possible to close the doors on yours.*

*Donna*

I went out to the caravan and told Mick he could come into the house to do some recordings and that he was to come alone.

Mick came to the door of the house in a fluffy top covered in boggledeeboo patterns. He was a big, jolly young man. He sat one step back inside his body, giving him a feel of being somehow a good deal older than his twenty-something years. Yet simultaneously he had an untouchability, like a child sitting somewhere in that adult's body, which had watched the world rather than letting it really connect with him. He stood biting his lip and basically looking lemony and like he was on the verge of disappearing himself. He tapped mousily at the door using the back of his big hand.

I presented myself in the doorway before going to walk off again with the assumption he'd follow. He stood there looking like he needed permission. I signalled for him to come inside and led him into the lounge room.

Mick set up his equipment on the floor, looking serious. Then he looked up at me and I looked back and we both smiled real smiles that rose right up into our eyes that had looked at each other with warmth. I realized I had made contact, personal contact, and I looked away. Shit, how did a Gadoodleborger get in here?

Gadoodleborgers were gatekeepers, bridgekeepers between what had once been the system of sensing which was the social, cognitive, emotional and perceptual reality of 'my world' and the system of interpretation by which, and in which, 'the worlders' lived. Gadoodleborgers were rare creatures, neither fully in 'their own world' nor in 'the world' but able to move between the two.

Ian entered the room and sat down on the chair in the corner to keep an eye out for me. I went to start reading my script, but the personal contact had made the exposure of reading out loud too hard to initiate now. I fluffed about a bit before starting.

When I finished reading, I looked up from the page and Mick caught my eyes, and an invisible warm breeze washed over me. In spite of the call of its comfort I looked away and defied the smile that had crept from my feelings up onto my face.

Loyally, I looked over at Ian, sitting on the chair in the corner as if to confirm to myself that I didn't piss on my own doorstep, that I knew who my special person was.

I had looked but felt no warm breeze. Instead, I felt myself looking for approval that all was OK, that nothing was going to get out of control, that Ian wouldn't let it.

In spite of myself, I found myself looking forward to the next day's filming when Mick would be here. It was OK, I told myself, he was 'like a brother'. It was just that I'd got hooked on the routine of working with him in the morning, and the security was wound up in that. Anyway, Mick was not 'my friend' but 'our friend', and I wasn't alone in wanting him to be in the house, Ian wanted him there too. Whilst Ian slept, I wrote him a letter and gave it to him when he got up.

*Hello Ian,*

*I haven't written you a letter for a long time. There's no trouble, just that what I felt and was thinking about can't get past the walls so I'm doing in writing what I can't otherwise say and discuss.*

*I find that I like Mick and I know you do too but neither of us are probably able to live that like in a fluently expressed way. I wondered if you felt OK to be 'friends' with Mick. He 'feels' to be a dependable solid self-honest person.*

*I feel that if something happened to one of us, he could be company with each of us as a brother might. I know we agreed that you'd have a dog and I'd get a caretaker in.*

*If you think he could be our friend, then I would like to give him a letter telling him that we feel he has a felt empathy with us and gives the 'feeling' that he feels us to be equals. I would write that I had wanted to tell him he is a welcome person and that I was curious to know how he lives and why someone who seems to live so differently seems to understand us from a felt inside understanding (not an outside studied understanding). I would ask him if he has known anyone else like us and if he would feel at all threatened to continue knowing us after the filming is done. I would tell him that he could leave us a business card through which we could contact him if we needed a 'friend' and if you wanted to, you could invite him here for what would probably be one of those uncomfortable lemony evening meals. He would probably like to get away from the others for an hour and might even like our company.*

*If he came to dinner, I would want to know about his house where he lives and who his friends are and if he feels happy with his life and if he feels other people understand him. I sense from him that he is very isolated and alone in this world, like he is watching a film but he is in it.*

*I would ask him if he writes to people and if he reads books and if he would like to drive a model car or fly a kite. I would like when he left to give him the Playdoh if you don't mind and if you agree to get him one.*

*That's all.*

*From Donna*

It was the next day of filming and Mick got out of the van and I hovered in the doorway. He was wearing the same fluffy top and I was staring at it, resonating with the feel it would have if patted.

'Boggledee, right?' said Mick, addressing me in my own language and tugging at the top. In silence, all I could do was nod before being compelled to go quickly back inside.

Having Mick come in to work with me first thing in the morning became a ritual during which time the rest of the crew sat out in the caravan feeling rejected and assuming it had something to do with their being Japanese. To them, it had seemed unfair. The director and the coordinator had read my books thoroughly and researched autism, making every effort to be understanding and friendly. Then, they'd all remained external by comparison with Mick.

After extensive checking, we invited Mick to dinner.

*Hello Mick,*

*We wanted to tell you that after today's filming you could drive the others home and if you wanted to, you could drive back to here for a while. We both checked and found we would like you to visit us as a person (as opposed to just in the job you do).*

*If you would like to visit us after the filming, Ian has some model cars and trucks that you probably saw and we checked and he would feel good if you wanted also to drive one when you visited. I've driven them. They are funny and quite wild. Also, Ian is a good cook and he would feel good to cook for the three of us if you wanted to stay for dinner.*

*We don't talk much socially — our 'social' is generally through other things. Ian reads novels so if you read books he would maybe talk about books. He also likes to hear about other places and we'd both like to know about where you live if you wanted to tell us. You are welcome to ask us questions about ourselves and to tell us lists of things about yourself and your life if you want to and feel comfortable to. Not all blah blah is awful and your pace, intonation, volume and format of speaking is fine for us.*

*Also, we did check what our feelings were and found we don't mind you playing the guitar. If you visited us and wanted to explore something, please don't worry. We are inviting you to our home (not for you compliantly to accept a request to be here) so what goes with that is that you should be free to be yourself here and not afraid to express an interest in whatever you are interested in.*

*If you did ask us if you could explore something then if you give us about 20 seconds, we would have enough time to process what we felt in response (most people expect you to know and respond in 1 second) and we could answer you from feelings and not just compliance.*

*Being around people like us just takes 'like' and a few minor adjustments in the mechanics of communication – but sometimes 'like' is rare and the minor adjustments are too much to ask of some people. We think you'll be OK with these things though.*

*That's all.*

*From Donna (and from Ian)*

Mick arrived and we all went outside. Ian busied himself with the vegetable patch. I stood by the fence where the sheep-lambs came over to say hi. Mick stood leaning on the fence a few feet along smoking a cigarette. We talked out loud to ourselves in response to each other and occasionally looked along the fence and caught each other's eyes. There was a familiarity so intense that it defied the fact we hardly knew each other.

As it got dark, we came inside and Ian cooked. We sat next to each other on one side of the dinner table with Mick, distanced, on the other.

I had lemons sitting facing Mick across the table, sharing in the same activity with him as we all ate, and it was hard to control my body and my noises as impulses fired all over the place. I could feel intensely who he was in every movement and every sound, and it was emotionally even harder for me because what I sensed was so inviting and resonated with me so intensely. I had never imagined anyone else could just walk into my heart like that, not since the Welshman all those years ago. But that was different, I had been in love with him and it was an impossible situation which could go nowhere: we had both been allergic to closeness.

'What's that for?' I asked pointing at the Guinness lapel pin he wore on his jacket every day.

'Guinness, mate,' said Mick. 'Wonderful stuff.'

'Yeah but what's the badge for?' I asked. 'Is it a kind of club?'

Mick laughed looking down at it a little embarrassed.

'Never really thought of it like that,' he said, 'just liked the badge.'

Dinner over, all three of us stood in the kitchen. I sat on the swing that hung from the ceiling of the sitting room just through the kitchen, swinging into the room they both stood in and back out again, back in again and back out again as I went through my list of questions that I had for Mick:

*Have you met any others like us before?*
*Do you live in a house or a flat?*
*Do you live with other people or not?*
*Do you have animals live with you?*
*Do you have brothers or sisters or not?*
*Are you friends with your parents or not?*
*What sort of things do you do?*
*Do you watch films or read books or not?*
*Do you ever write letters or postcards?*
*Do you like Wales and would you visit Wales by choice?*
*Do you compose music or just play it?*

Mick lived in a shared house with mates in Newcastle having left his two dogs back in Ireland. He had three sisters, no brothers, loved his mother and had loved his big-drinking father who had died a few years back. He spent his spare time in pubs and out clubbing with his mates. He was dyslexic, had struggled with passing English, barely sent a letter or postcard in his life and didn't read much except the occasional newspaper column in the tabloids he'd pick up on a train. He loved Wales, which reminded him of Ireland. He had grown up in Dublin, but moved to the UK for work and landed in Newcastle because it was cheaper than London. He played guitar badly but knew a few tunes on a fiddle if he had one, which he didn't.

I got Mick to list me good smells, good things to touch, good things to eat, things that make good noises and things with good colours and patterns, and I gave him my list and Ian contributed some of his, and I whooped and buzzed from the sensory associations.

I was a cat and Mick had the feel of an open fire. It was OK, I told myself, it was like having a brother with none of the complications of my background and, besides, Ian liked him too. Still, it nagged me that it didn't feel so with Ian, and it nagged at me that there was a silent and intuitive Gadoodleborgonian non-verbal dialogue going on between Mick and me. Moreover, when I watched him with Ian, in spite of their friendliness towards each other that was all there was. There was no drawing force, no warm fire.

I looked over at Ian and guilt gripped me. Intermittently Mick would catch my eyes and the warmth would slap it down. I searched Ian's eyes more, held his hand more and smelled him more, like the cat with the familiar cushion that it tries to make comfortable.

I would miss Mick when the filming was over. I would miss him almost unbearably. I wondered about his life way out there somewhere in the world and how I would feel sat propped on a bar stool next to him with his Guinness. I wished he lived near so I could visit and have a cup of tea.

The next day we went out filming. Mick had been out for a few pints at the local pub that night and had nightmares all night about being real and being false. His face was serious and absorbed as he focused on his job, becoming part of it as I did when in the grip of a musical composition or the writing of a book. Then I would look at him and he'd look back and his entire humanness would break out through his body and his face and he'd look at me, biting his lip like he was caught between two worlds. Because I felt safe with him, I relaxed more with the rest of the crew too, being less rigid with the structure I had set out for the documentary, being less inflexible and more accommodating of their suggestions and loosening my grip on routine. They were getting in on his meal ticket.

I stood out in the courtyard dropping pebbles onto other pebbles and listening for the perfect 'clack' where two pebbles hit with a strong and substantial tone, playing like a whole note. Mick stood nearby trying it for himself.

'Here, try this one,' he said as though out loud to himself, feeling he had found a really good one.

I took the pebble from him, compelled to avoid any direct contact and dropped it onto the pebbles below. It hit with a good substantial 'clack' and I smiled, picking the pebble up and returning it to him before being driven to rush back inside. Later, when I came out again, the pebble was sitting just inside the front porch, seemingly left for me in an indirectly confrontational way, just as my father used to leave objects for discovery within my world.

The next day of filming, we travelled out to a seaside resort town. It was dusk, and the director and the coordinator had their own needs regarding the day's filming. It was clear these sometimes made no sense of my reality and felt foreign and wrong and rushed. The cameraman was enthusiastic and as eager as ever in the chaos of demand and expectation. Mick was tense in spite of the facade of friendliness he had put upon his face. Ian, like me, was lost and becoming compliant.

I had never seen Mick so self-betraying like this. I resonated with him and hurt for it. He looked tied up in there and I felt compelled to free him. His obvious 'no' gave rise to my 'yes' and, freed momentarily from my Exposure Anxiety, I ignored everyone else and walked over to him and addressed him directly.

'Are you angry?' I asked.

'No. Not at all,' he replied, his eyes looking caught and his body and face taking on a stored role of friendliness in denial of what was clearly a distressed feel to this man.

'Are you upset?' I asked, thinking I must have got it wrong.

'No. I'm just tired,' replied Mick looking edgy.

His eyes were reaching out but also begging to be let off the hook as the rest of the crew looked on, observing this caring personal directness that they had never had the privilege to be the recipients of. His 'no' shouted loudly in the silence and my 'yes' competed. I took charge and silenced myself.

Ian and I continued to walk down the street as dusk crept into night, and I felt like breaking into a run. I knew Mick was in hiding but didn't know why. Was he hiding from me and if so, what had I done to cause him such mistrust?

Ian and I had walked off from the crew, and Mick had also walked away from the others. He came up to us and we all leaned over the rail at the edge of the night ocean, which swayed below us with a gentle roar as it crashed its fluid blackness against the wall below like a big glass of Guinness pouring out.

Mick explained that I'd been right and that he was upset, but that he couldn't show it in front of the rest of the crew back there. He had felt a big empathy for the pressure being put on us and for the effect of the chaos we were caught up in with such weighty expectations.

After one month, my twelve-page schedule for the documentary was coming to a close. Mick would be going and there was a deep sadness in the air.

'Last time we work together today,' said Mick without a shred of relief.

I knew how he felt.

The final recording was called 'About going', and I'd written it as a way of getting some of my feelings out. It read:

> People assume that if you've spent time together with other people, you will have built up rapport with them over time. Unless you've disliked the people, it is assumed some sort of relationship has evolved. This assumption works fine for people who get to know each other through the system of interpretation. For them, each new meeting brings more knowing.

> I don't use interpretation to build relationships. Over time I just accumulate a larger store of facts and establish some routines involving people's ongoing presence. When the people leave, I retain that impersonal, factual information, even for years and years, along with all other personally irrelevant information that my undiscriminating brain picks up. When the people leave, it is the end of the routine and that can be jolting. As long as I have disassembled all established routines by the time the people go, I'm generally not bothered.

> Very occasionally I'll deeply connect with someone who's entered my life. To me that's like a good dinner or like a picture that I like so I'm not indifferent to seeing good things go. But this has to do with sensing. I will sense whether I feel right around someone in a few seconds so if I don't find that with someone in a few seconds, then knowing them for a week or a month or a year won't change that.

I managed to ask Mick for his card in case we could ask him to work with us on another documentary some time. He said he'd be glad to come back. As I hid behind Ian, we asked if he would come back for dinner again before he headed back and he said that would be good.

The filming was over and the crew all left. I felt sad for them. It had mattered so much to them for me to like them personally and want to get to know them. But they were very self-in-relation-to-other and I was essentially self-in-relation-to-self. There must have been families like this, all of one type with one the odd one out. We were as different as dogs and cats, and I'd found no want in me. No matter how much they liked me, they'd never be able to put their minds to one side and just feel who I was. Nor would they easily know what it was just to let their real selves emerge wild, expressive and free beyond their deeply cemented rigidity and stored learning. Being 'good people' won you politeness and friendliness, but it didn't win you closeness.

Mick arrived the next morning and he and I seemed like a sorry pair. Ian was relieved it was all over and was looking forward to 'getting our lives back' as he put it.

As Mick left, his movements made him look like he had to prise himself away from the place. He had found peace here. We had agreed to call one another just to say hi sometime. Although I didn't do that sort of thing, I wondered if maybe in all the dared exposure of the documentary that I couldn't just find it in me now. Mick had agreed that it wouldn't matter if I called with nothing to say or unable to say anything. It would be good anyway.

My father had been on my mind. It had been about seven months since I'd seen him for that brief twenty minutes, the first time in five years. I had always been incredibly private even when seemingly public, but I had the nagging feeling for some intangible reason that it was important right now for him to know some things about my life. I wanted him to have a picture in his mind of where and how I lived, for him to know I was OK. Ian could see no point in it and felt cautious about me 'inviting him into my life', but nothing he could say could stop the gripped feeling in my stomach. I had to send my father some pictures for his mind. I wrote to him.

*Hello Jackie Paper,*

*Here's some photos, one of our house, one of some of the farmer's sheep in our field and one of the garden at the side of the house.*

*Our house is made of big stones and it is 500 years old – quite usual for around here. It is a traditional house, very much the same as many houses nearby. It's called a Welsh Farmhouse. It's basically a big lego block with rooms inside and a staircase in the middle. The land around here is farmland and very green most of the time but in the summer when the hay is cut it looks a bit like Australia.*

*Along the roads there are no fences, just hedges that keep the sheep in their fields so you drive along not seeing much of the land. There are rabbits and we saw a fox yesterday. He was elegant and I'd never seen one. He was like a cat-dog.*

*The trees are big and chunky, like oak and maple trees and there's no twiggy gum trees. The trees all go bare in winter and then it snows on tree-skeletons. The trees go to sleep and wake up again in the spring and grow buds and leaves.*

*The birds are dainty and twittering, not at all squawking birds. Few magpies and they don't speak the same as Australian ones at all. There are crows and jackdaws. There are swallows which dart everywhere and wild finches. Ian feeds them.*

*We grow vegetables in a greenhouse and in a garden we dug up. We have all sorts and some baby fruit trees. We are eating our lettuce, our potatoes, our peas and our spinach at the moment.*

*That's all.*

*From Donna (and Ian)*

Jackie Paper was terrified of flying and had never been on a plane. He had a great deal of difficulty in writing a letter but still I received one straight back written all in capitals with no punctuation and spelling and phrasing that often took some time to work out.

*Dear Daughter,*

*Thankyou for the card I got yesterday. The roses and the garden look nice. The Government just declared three states drought effected. Almost all my sheep are gone now and the business had to close because it was losing too much money to keep going. Thankyou for the surprise visit. You should have wrote or rang to say you were coming. Did Ian like Australia? Did you go far on your holiday? Did you see Western Australia or Alice Springs? Thanks for the kind words you wrote about me but sometimes in my life I was not worthy of such statements of kindness. But however some people say you improve with age so I must be coming good. Donna in this world of ours all people are supposed to be equal and peaceful but I think I got it mixed up and thought it meant jealous and spiteful so care for yourself and you will be a survivor and not a loser. I have often said I am brilliant and as long as I believe myself I must be. I went out dancing with my new lady on Saturday night and I get all the love and affection that was lacking elsewhere. She says one of her daughters is similar to you in ways so don't laugh about that. You're not on your own. I know you worry that I was alone back in the years when there was so much horror and you should know that I wasn't. I had a lady friend then, not one I slept with, but like a social worker, she was. I had somewhere to go and used to sneak off there about once a week for nearly ten years. I wanted you just to know that there were some good people out there who took care of me. I hope you are enjoying yourself overseas. Enjoy it, don't waste it by putting too much faith in others. Sometimes trusting people it does not work out. I miss you and wish you were back. I am finished with the Chemotherapy for now and I may write a book about cancer. Its surprising there's not a lot of knowledge around about it. At different times, I lend your books to my friends, namely at the hospital. They have been very impressed with it and I feel very proud.*

*Thankyou for writing and communicating with me over the last few months. It has had the correct feeling towards family and on some nights it has taken away the loneliness and stress and can make one smile as he writes. Please don't think I am going crazy in this letter. Its only me.*

*Please excuse the writing but it is a long time since I have written letters to anyone and to me they must be something special to me for me to do so.*

*Hope you and the lambs are happy. I know its too late for Easter but I enclose a cheque for you so you can get an Easter Egg.*

*Love from Jackie Paper.*

There were just six weeks until the filming of a Canadian documentary would start. The intense involvement with the Japanese film crew over one month had brought out so much in me and I was hungry for the classroom of life.

At night, we'd lie down on the sofa to watch a film as always, but more and more it became hard for Ian to get me to come and lie with him. I had got past the 'let me help you get over your problems with touch' thing. But beyond dependency there was no gut-level closeness to sustain us as a couple, and I had none of the drive of physical attraction. Now, to my shock, I was finally, progressively, developing these feelings, but not for him.

Ian sat with the receipts, talking about how much more money was due from book sales and the future film based on the books. Having bought the house and filled it, bought the car and various playthings, he had got interested recently in investments. On his advice, I'd bought property and placed it in the hands of an estate agent to rent so there'd be some money to live off as the book royalties would inevitably fade with time.

I had told Ian that I wanted to help my younger brother out. But Ian would continually remind me how we couldn't afford it and how such things would have to wait until after we had enough investments to pay all the bills, including expensive bills like the solicitor and the accountant. Eventually, even these bills seemed taken care of and I put it to him again. It would have to wait, he told me, we needed to have enough investments for what we called 'thrills and spills' money: the money that would cover things like trips to Australia every so often, or in case we got sick.

Ian was proud of our house and the land it lived in. He felt strong and safe driving the car, not just because it was structurally safe, but because its prestige, in his perception, somehow scared people in some way. He felt people respected him more, and he found strength in that like so many people do.

Something had changed in Ian since buying investment property. Suddenly, when I would go to buy something, he would remind me to be careful with money. It would just be a cheap hair tie that made me smile and buzz, a small plastic container of buzzy paper clips that made a great noise, or a cat magazine, and he would remind me to be careful about money. I would tell him there'd be more coming in and he would remind me that all the big money had already come in, all that would come in now would be little money and there was no certainty the film would end up being made because all sorts of things could happen. 'Don't count on money you don't have,' he would say. Yet he was still buying model aircraft at £500 each, which crashed to the ground before the purchase of a new one, a ride-on lawn mower, remote control cars, and an architectural draftsman's drawing board.

In the few weeks since Mick had been with us, he had become a symbol of hope, an invisible comrade in what had become the starchy atmosphere of a cardboard cut-out of a marriage. With Ian's agreement, I had spoken to Mick in his shared house in Newcastle, a world away.

Mick answered the phone with a put-on voice that had no natural 'him' in it. In that two seconds I could hear that the tone of his inner self was overlaid. He reeled off a kind of 'am I creating the desired cool impression'. This socially manipulative style, so clearly 'self-in-relation-to-other' was like fingernails down a blackboard to someone like me. I lived in a world dominated by sensing. In that tone was the superficiality of those I saw as 'the worlders', people who cared about making an impression and controlling the responses of others. I stuttered a bit, unsure of what to say and unsure that Mick was everything I remembered him to be. Had I done it again – had I focused on the part and lost sight of the whole?

I asked if he had been having fun. He talked about people having taken over his room, having drunk his wine, about getting pissed and falling off his bar stool, casting these comments off as though I might judge them, a kind of 'do you really want to know?' I did really want to know and after he'd finished distancing me, he began to warm till we were laughing. Ian kept an eye from the kitchen. It had been hard for Mick since the filming. It had shaken him up. His voice got a bit shaky and he told me it had been hard to leave the Simply Be feel of how things were in Wales and return to 'the world' expectations, roles and social game playing now no longer so easy to stomach, or so unquestionable. I told him I was sorry. He said not to worry about it, that it had been an amazing experience, he'd been glad to have it, even if it now made life more difficult.

There was the Canadian documentary to make and I had asked them if they would use him on the crew and they had agreed. Ian had been unsure about having Mick come back, saying maybe I should work with someone else this time. But it had been my want to have him back and I had no cause to question why. I didn't ask Ian to check.

Mick was glad to be coming back and I was glad too. Inside of me it was as though I had had news that my best friend was arriving after years away. Ian was looking forward to getting the whole thing over with, and he seemed to be the last person I could share this happiness with. I kept it to myself with an attitude of 'that's nice'.

The day before filming, the director, a lovely, lanky Canadian named Steve, arrived to meet us. He was quiet and controlled, his emotions stifled to a whisper. I had a feeling about him that was nothing but good. From the moment he came in, there was something familiar about him. His pace, movements and tone were somehow formal, a little Aspergerian.

Ian had noticed it too and had warmed to this man instantly, finding a new spark of interest connected with this documentary. For once, Ian was not indifferent to the visitor, nor did he want him to go. The man was clearly a fellow comrade, and Ian flitted about after him, giggly and alive like I had never seen him with anyone.

The next day. Steve and Mick showed up ready to start filming. We were all polarized. As strongly as I had taken to the familiarity of Mick, Ian had taken to Steve.

I fell straight back into my old structure and everything was going according to script. Being already familiar with the structure and working with two people who spoke my own behavioural language, I felt so at ease with this relaxed 'Simply Being' crew.

These were good days. The sun was shining, the butterflies were out and the ladybirds crawled over long curving blades of grass. Mick and Steve lay on the grass in the sunshine in the breaks between filming, drinking coffee as Mick rolled cigarettes. I 'visited' with them, attempting to converse, but more often being compelled to make diversions into unconnected little statements of fact, making little grass sculptures, finding good leaves and collecting good-sounding rocks as I related as I could in an indirectly-confrontational way and everyone made me feel so tremendously 'normal'. Just hovering around them as they did their thing, simply being, I felt with 'family', like I was in someone's backyard with people I was safe with and who accepted me as an equal.

But dark clouds began to hover within me as something progressively kept knocking on the doors of consciousness, demanding awareness that on breaks between filming, I felt more belonging out with Mick than I did inside in the space I shared with Ian. It was worse than this. I actually felt progressively safer and freer without Ian present than when he was.

No longer needed as my caretaker, Ian progressively became more and more casual about the filming. 'Am I in this part?' he would ask in order to confirm that he was free to go and get on with more interesting things.

I felt for Ian, but even more strongly, I felt for me. There was an ever-increasing feeling that my freedom was Ian's suffocation. We began having fights every day or so.

The fights were about everything but about nothing in particular. I didn't even see them as fights, I saw them as 'attacks of defensiveness'. I had no idea what I had done wrong or why I had been so bad. I tried to point out that this defensiveness, this picking, was driving me crazy, that it confused me, made me feel suffocated, made me eager to please and compliant in relation to him. I didn't know why Ian needed such power, such control, or why I seemed to be the target. I knew he didn't mean the defensiveness, but in such states he lost all link to any gentler emotions and no remnant remained of felt empathy, no capacity to simultaneously take account of his own chosen 'side' within the context of my life too.

I had a creeping feeling I didn't want to face. Ian had had all the investments put into his own name, arguing that it made good tax sense. Something had empowered him. I checked.

'Why are you doing this?' I asked.

'What?' he replied.

'Ian is doing this because he's got the investments in his name,' I stated watching for the response.

The glint in his eye threw me and cheekiness came through his mouth and jaw as he struggled to stifle his emotional recognition of this truth. Fuck, I thought, I'm in deep shit.

When the crew would appear, he would smile and drop his defensiveness and all would look sweetness and light. It was making me crazy and my only empowerment was my capacity publicly, and without apology, to expose it for what it was so he'd be forced to take personal responsibility for it and assess whether or not he wanted to side with his difficulties or fight them. I refused to hide it from the crew that we'd been fighting, and refused to just carry on as if nothing had happened. I couldn't smile when I'd felt mentally and emotionally overloaded and harassed for several hours and was then expected to pretend I was just fine and ready to get on with filming.

It was 6am and I couldn't sleep late. My mind was full and I had to go and play with plastic cows to hold on to my thoughts and see where they were going. I sat downstairs with four hours till the crew would arrive and played out all my thinking through the cows, making them represent positive points and negative points. With a little over a week till our second wedding anniversary, I had some tidying to do regarding my marriage. I wanted to get things straight in my head even if I had to work it all out outside of my head to do so. When I understood I went to the computer and typed everything out so I could hand my thinking to Ian.

*OUR GOOD POINTS AS A COUPLE:*

*We are a working team – in touring, and dealing with business.*

*We live together as housepartners very well and fit into each other's routines and allow each other private space as good housepartners should and appreciate our shared desire to live a safe, non 'the world', life.*

*We are friends who try our hardest to understand and support each other as friends no matter what.*

*We are committed to each other.*

OUR BAD POINTS AS A COUPLE:

*We share some information processing problems – and the consequences of this for lostness in the sea of other, but this is only half our battle. The other half for each of us is strikingly different – your other half hangs upon things being 'ready', 'controlled', 'proper,' my other half hangs upon total realness at all times. It is these halves that clash brutally.*

*In me, I have some of this need to prepare and be constantly 'ready', to be 'controlled' and 'proper' but this is a distant part of me that I can't live compatibly with or it would take over and strangle the life out of me. So, I fight to govern this fear of losing control and I'm committed to that fight.*

*It is possible for you to be 'real' but you are not so emotionally hypersensitive that you CANNOT HELP but be real even in a world which is not. Whilst you can appreciate realness, you are not forced to live there and when it slips from you, you can't even remember your realness until you are back again.*

*It is this other half of me, this inescapable realness that runs in my blood and is my air. It is this other half of you – this insatiable quest to hold controlled, predictable perfection – that governs all that you find harmonious, from your models to your sketches to the way you wash yourself.*

*We have fought each other brutally for what comes naturally to ourselves and in the process have brought out in each other that hidden part of ourselves – the potential perfectionist in me, and the real person in you. We have also caused self-hate to run deep in each of us – you hateful of your defensive need to prepare, control and retain perfection, me hateful of the klutsy reckless freedom in me that comes with brutal realness and cognitive simplicity. It is this part of us that needs to find not just acceptance, but sameness – where trust comes not with 'effort' but simply in knowing these things come naturally to someone else too. This is what you find in Steve. This is what I find in Mick.*

*Just as you would like to spend time alone with people like Steve, I would like to spend time on my own with Mick. If it ever happened that some time I wanted to spend social time together with Mick, then I would like to meet with him just as you might have wanted to spend time on your own with Steve. Mick and I could meet somewhere, and you shouldn't be scared for me to have this freedom because*

*I would always be here to live with my friend, brother, workpartner and housepartner – you. Mick lives among 'the worlders' in a way I never could. This is why my home is with you.*

*We opened the door for each other and showed each other we could find a place we could stay and build as a safe place without aloneness. Those are good things. Yet though I am married to you, I have never felt to be anyone's wife and always felt right to use my own name. Sometimes I tried to say that or show it, but it wasn't your want so it got stifled. Though you feel secure married to me, I know you do not feel husbandly either. And it's OK.*

*Mick and I are like IBM and you are like Apple Macintosh. We are/were the lost without belonging who found each other and had the love that a child has for its friend – IBM and Apple Macintosh in an Amstrad world. Give the IBM or AppleMac a spaceship to travel to be with even one of its own kind and ask would the IBM and Apple forget each other and the comradeship of being aliens together in this world, albeit from different planets? They would not forget each other, but nor would they have it in their hearts to disassemble or disregard the spaceship no matter how loudly the Amstrad word 'should' may shout – there are higher laws.*

*So there it is . . .*

*Donna*

After breakfast and before the film crew arrived, Ian went down to the gate to get the post. It was the length of a two-acre field and back and took about ten minutes to walk there and return. I stayed calm. From the kitchen window, I saw him out of view and raced for the phone. I phoned my accountant and whispered to be put through urgently. I spoke quickly, explaining I was in an emergency. I explained he was not to send anything or phone back but should arrange for the name on all investments to be returned to my name alone.

'Are you alright?' asked my accountant.

'I can't talk now,' I replied. 'He's just down at the post box, he doesn't know I'm calling.'

My accountant understood. He would fix it.

July had turned to August as we headed towards the end of the first week of the filming. I was sitting outside on the grass with Mick and Steve when Ian came outside to join us. He had just received a phone call.

My literary agent had called to let me know my older brother had called. My father was in hospital. He had developed the late stages of cancer of the pancreas and liver and had somewhere between a few days to two weeks to live.

I called my older brother. He knew that my father had been MY parent far more than his or my younger brother's. He knew that if I had any say it wouldn't have been Jackie Paper to go first, that it would have been my mother to go so I would have had some time to spend with my father, unthreatened by potential contact with or control by her. He knew that of all of us it was I who'd feel the loss most.

'Don't be upset with yourself,' I told my older brother.

He seemed confused.

'Just don't be surprised if you feel relief that he's going,' I went on. 'He's been a major part of the war in this family. There can't be any more war when one side has gone.'

One parent was alcoholic, severe, calculating, agoraphobic, obsessive-complusive, yet Aspergerian; the other flamboyant, manic-depressive, a binge drinker, colourful, funny, dyslexic and ADD. Yet both were violent, captivating and larger than life in their own ways. For thirty-two years there'd been a dividing line down the family, dividing me and my father from my brothers and mother on the other side. Now that my father was dying, he would no longer be caught up in power plays with my mother and we'd no longer feel like pawns in their use of their children in infantile battles, emotional blackmail, one-upmanship and the, often one-sided, verbal abuse that had gone on long after the physical abuse of both parties had petered out. The monster would no longer be taunted by the victim it couldn't keep down, and the victim would no longer be made righteous by the monster's dark and often dangerous compulsive defensiveness.

I called my father.

'Hiya, Polly,' he said in a whisper of a voice, its strength stolen by the silent thief of cancer.

'Hi, Jackie Paper,' I replied, something in me almost exploding knowing this was our last time together and it would be over a telephone.

'Don't be scared of death, Jackie Paper,' I told him. 'You are going to fly.'

'I'm not scared any more, Miss Polly,' he replied in a struggling whisper. 'I know and I'm looking forward to it.'

'I want to play something for you,' I said.

I put the receiver on my lap and, sitting at the piano, played a piece I'd composed called 'Stars'. My hands shook, in the grip of Exposure Anxiety, but I played in spite of them. It was a piece that was fragile and delicate but powerful and moving. I returned to the phone.

'You just made an old man cry,' said my young 58-year-old father who wouldn't make 60.

He was crying. I'd never seen or heard him cry.

'I love you, Donna,' he said.

I considered the words and replied, without compliance, the words I'd never said to him: 'I love you too, Dad,' wiping tears away.

'I won't be going to the funeral. Is that OK?' I asked.

'It's not the place for you. I don't want you to go there,' he replied.

And I knew that he knew me.

I told him I wouldn't be making contact with my mother.

'I understand that Polly. You're being sensible. You keep yourself safe,' he said, finally relaying to me a feeling that went beyond him being Jackie Paper.

He had spoken to me as a father. He was dying and his spirit was going to fly. I was glad for him. He would be free. I said goodbye to him and thanked God for the gift of a death that lets one say one's goodbyes and make peace. Then I phoned the florist and had them send him flowers that he could see with living eyes before he went. I sent bright, bold colours like the person inside of him, and I asked the florist to send them with a note which read 'Happy flying'.

It was just over a week later at the end of a series of warm and beautiful short chats with a man progressively struggling for the energy even to speak or breathe when Ian took another call. He came outside and told me to sit down. My father, Jackie Paper, had gone flying. My older brother had put one of the flowers in his hands to take with him for the journey. It had taken all my life to speak to Jackie Paper with feelings and self in shared dialogue, and now I would never speak to him again. And I had never told him what I'd so wanted to let go. Never told him, but had written it in a poem in a book dedicated to him for his support as fellow war comrade in the 15-year sentence of my childhood. I'd sent the book by post, so wanting him to know the truth was freed and that he had been such a strength and inspiration, whatever his darknesses. The poem of what had happened to him all those years ago back in his thirties when the word cancer was first being bandied about would reach his girlfriend's house a week after his death and he would never know. I would never know for sure whether his cancer had really begun back in his thirties when he began to lose weight dramatically and develop the bowel problems I'd heard so gloatingly discussed in celebratory tones by another voice in that house. I would never hear that it was OK, that I was forgiven for helping to stir the gravy which went onto his plate night after night with me able to say nothing as he ate the food covered by gravy, stirred by the daughter he trusted.

Mick and Steve sat across from me on the grass. In my hand I had a cup full of water. Tears fell silently from my eyes in floods and the world looked misty and dreamlike. I stood and tossed the contents as high into the air as I could toss them. The droplets flew wildly like smooth silver crystals up into the sunlight and the blue sky. I shouted out into the wind with all my heart and soul. 'Goodbye Jackie Paper!'

Ian's mother had died, and his indifference to her loss was a reflection of the indifference she had had to him as a boy she could not relate to. Mick's father had spent much of his life at the pub and was his icon, and he'd loved him very much. When he had died from cancer, Mick had never felt he had spent enough time with him. Ian knew that as much as he felt for my pain, he couldn't share this with me. Mick reached out to me with his eyes and we talked of death and what death meant and of loss of imperfect but loved people and how it felt and where Jackie Paper had gone.

The next three days of filming were interspersed every so often with tears as I reflected on one thing or another about my father. Whenever I used objects to hold thoughts together or communicate through, he was there. Whenever I attributed responsibility to my shoes or the glass or the fork or the jacket in order to get me to the toilet, have that drink, eat that food or put on that jacket in the grip of Exposure Anxiety, he was there. Whenever I buzzed about sounds, patterns or the play of light upon something, he was there. When I laughed, he was in my laugh. When I smiled, I had his dancing eyes. I was filled with such regret and with relief that finally I was free from contact with my family if ever I wanted it that way. Relief, too, that now I was free to remember him in my own world, in my own way, that he had left his body but was somehow now a stronger, more celebrated presence within myself.

Whatever else he was, he was the man who made animals and objects speak so that where I could not dare to speak directly, I could speak through them, as them and to them. He was the wild euphoric madman whose eyes would flash and would announce he was Elvis or Jesus, that he could hypnotize cats or cure cancer. He was the laughing maniac who tied me and my younger brother to the clothes line to spin us around and around and who scooped the fish out of the fish pond, flinging the contents of the net into the clear chlorinated pool so I could swim with the fishes and who fed the dog Kit Kat's insisting the German sheppard suck them and not bite them, who would chase you wildly with a piece of snot and build a playhouse like only a five-year-old could. He was the dangerous crazy man on a bender who would suddenly veer the car off the road, taking us screaming and terrified straight through the grassy park and circling around the trees as he opened his driver's door to half fly, half drive, euphorically buzzing with his body half out the door, his foot full down on the accelerator and one hand on the steering wheel and no idea of consequences. He was the nutter who suddenly jumped from the car, climbed a wire fence into someone's car yard and danced on the car bonnets. He was the naughty flasher who occasionally flashed himself at female guests visiting our house but who just as quickly could turn into something closer to Jack Nicholson in the film *The Shining*. He was the man who had jumped on tables to break into song as all manner of performers, totally in his own world, and was also the man who had left me a record player in late childhood, allowing me exploration in my own time and way eventually to sing along with all manner of performers in the prison cell of my room. It was he who so loved my songs and voice he'd jumped up on stage with a home-made tape of me singing to give it to the members of a local band in a pub in his town, to tell them 'that's my daughter on there'. He was the man who had left oil paints, brushes and a canvas in my room in my late childhood to be discovered, and I'd eventually painted my first painting and hidden it in the roof where he'd never seen it, nevertheless, aware I was known, that I was alive and expressive. He was the one who had left a typewriter in my room for me to discover when I was nine, and without which I would never have learned that where I could not speak interpersonally, I could speak to myself via typing. He was the man so proud of my books and writing, he'd displayed them on top of his cabinets and loaned them to the nurses in the hospital. He had read my children's book, about the adventures of a weed which had been ripped up out of the ground into a big adventure before finding a sense of home again. He had loved it and believed in it, certain it would one day bring happiness to people. He was the man to whom I had shown my poetry and who found it beautiful. He had a generosity of spirit which was infectious in his storytelling, his laughter, his daring and surrealism, in spite of, perhaps because of, the war zone we'd shared in the house I had grown up in. Though I fought the worst of his manic-depressive tendencies within myself, though I'd inherited a brain with a slipped gear for an attention span, though I'd inherited the frustration of dyslexia in a literate world, I had no regrets. I was his daughter, whatever other monster of a husband he had been to my equally monstrous mother. His death was an ending and with it came the pain and invitation to adventure that is change. Yet he would never be gone as long as I celebrated his existence within me.

I'd woken from a jolting dream in which I had been inside a house. In the dream I had been standing in a room and there were sparkles, like glitter, on the floor. There was a spinning top, and I picked it up and took it to the centre of the floor and then spun it. As it spun, it set the glitter off into sparks which flew wildly like mini fireworks. Suddenly, I heard an enormous approaching thundering sound as if a tornado or earthquake was coming. I ran to the window in an adjoining room to look out and see what was approaching. A huge bomb, like a nuclear bomb, went off and in a split second fire suddenly raced outwards across the horizon as far as the eye could see and tore straight for the house in a matter of seconds. I turned from the window running as fast as I could back to the room where the sparkles were. Mick and Ian were both there, as though waiting for me. Quickly, I grabbed for their hands, the three of us standing in something of a magic circle. 'Goodbye,' I said in that final urgent second. Then all was gone.

Tomorrow was a day off. It was my and Ian's second wedding anniversary. Before the end of the working day, Ian had asked Steve if he could borrow his camcorder. They had brought one along in case there was something I had wanted to film and Ian had decided to use it on our anniversary.

We didn't know what people did on anniversaries. We had only invited three people to the wedding and all of them were in the one family and we'd included no-one else. So in spite of how well known I was, our wedding anniversary went basically unremembered by anyone other than us.

We agreed to get dressed up in our wedding clothes. We had meant to do it the year before but somehow hadn't got around to it.

Our anniversary had a lonely and fragile feel to it, like we were shells or husks from a field of grain about to be blown away by the first sign of an erratic wind.

Ian set the camcorder going. He filmed every room in the house and all of our belongings. He filmed me eating a breakfast he had made me and filmed the pony and the pigs and the sheep out in the fields. It seemed like the sort of thing someone did when someone was going to die in order to leave memories behind, like the kind of home video you take out and look at after a death.

'Is this a goodbye video?' I said looking up from my breakfast and making blatant the feel to this strange scene.

Once we'd put on our wedding clothes, he filmed me in them out in the sunshine but showed no interest in being filmed in his. The focus was on me.

'We have to have someone see us in our wedding clothes,' Ian announced.

Nobody known to us but our three wedding guests had seen us and now suddenly it was important that someone did. Ian suggested we go around to the hotel where Mick was staying and show him our wedding clothes. In the eerie feel of the day, the sunshine that offered sounded like a good idea.

We got into the car, me tucking in all the flounce of the billowing wedding dress, and drove the five minutes around the corner to where Mick and Steve were staying. We got out of the car and went to Mick's door and knocked. With a very lemony expression on his face, he invited us in.

I felt deeply exposed in my off-the-shoulder dress with a crown of peach silk flowers on my head, looking about as feminine and vulnerable as I ever had in this life. I sat on the spare bed in his room and Ian sat next to me.

'So these are your wedding clothes,' said Mick hurriedly putting out a cigarette and not really knowing how to handle all of this. That made two of us.

'This is the last time I'll wear these clothes,' said Ian.

Mick seemed surprised, put on the spot. With hesitation he asked Ian why. Ian replied: 'Well, they won't fit me after this year, unless I get Aids or something.' It was a bizarre comment. A bizarre comment on a bizarre day.

We hadn't stayed long and I was glad to leave. I had felt nude and somehow out of control of the whole presentation, as though I was not presenting myself as much as my husband was presenting me: his wife.

Filming was arranged for the following day, of a woman now married two years in the eyes of the law. I woke up and snuggled up to Ian. We had about two hours before the crew showed up and there was a physical closeness between us that had been absent for some time. It was good to see it back.

I got up and attempted to make myself breakfast. Ian came downstairs and joined me.

'I've decided to leave,' he said.

I couldn't believe what I was hearing. I had seen no signs of it and I couldn't put this together with the man who had seemed to care so much for me, to whom it seemed I meant the world. Even now, there was no coldness, no animosity.

I felt sick and nauseous. I couldn't believe this could happen, just four days after my father dying.

'I don't understand,' I said. 'Why?'

'It's just too hard to be real anymore,' Ian replied calmly, almost casually.

Five minutes ticked by, ten minutes ticked by, fifteen minutes ticked by. Then Ian went on to raise the issue of finances. We had been married two years now, he explained. He was entitled to half of everything and that's what he wanted. In plain simple language, he wanted half of everything and if I didn't like that he would wait till the film of my books was made when there'd be plenty more.

I now understood. Ian had stood there and said: 'But my defences ARE me and I'm them. It's all part of Ian.' I had seen that he was disconnected from his actions. I had thought: 'Surely, he does not actually intend or want to go against his real self?' If the same had happened within me, I would have felt my real self screaming and fighting against the self-denial of such disconnected actions. For me, my defences were not 'me'. For Ian, they were. What I hadn't understood was that the critical point was about want: whether one wanted to be untrue to one's true feelings. It was about identity and what one identified with. Perhaps he had two sets of feelings – one I convinced myself was his real set because it suited me to think so, but the other was just as much him, should the mood take him to swing that way. And suddenly I began not just to understand Ian, but to understand my nemesis ten thousand miles away: my mother.

I knew what it was to be compelled to go against your own true feelings and be unable to defy the unwanted and unintentional sellout. I now saw that people could actually intentionally choose to defy their real feelings and, more brutally, that living with me in a situation in which he was constantly forced to be true to his real self, Ian had found our relationship far from delivering the freedom it stood for. It had been a constant battle and a tiring one. To fight for something without equal fire within to match the decided commitment makes it hard work regardless of the rewards. For me, freedom meant defying all compulsion to sell out and, no matter what, be free to be your true self at any cost. For Ian, freedom had a different definition.

Two hours later, the crew showed up to start the day's filming, Mick and Steve smiling, glad to see us. It seemed macabre.

Ian came with me out to the caravan. He showed no signs of what had gone on and continued to chat with them as though it was just another day. I could hardly believe that it was going to go ahead like this – like any other day. I had that 'stop the world, I want to get off' feeling and I let it be known.

'There's some things I have to talk about before we go on,' I said, interrupting Steve's spiel about the plans for the day's filming. 'If I don't deal with this, I'm going to be sick.'

I then told Ian to take Steve with him and tell him what had happened, and I would stay and tell Mick.

Mick had been cutting down on smoking and was proud of himself for it. I sat down on the grass, and Mick sat on the steps of the caravan.

'Ian's leaving me,' I told him as I started to cry.

Mick's hands had tremors as he reached for his cigarettes, stuck one in his face and drew deeply on it.

'He says he wants half of everything.' I went on, crying some more.

Mick looked like a stunned fish.

'That's not the worst of it,' I went on. 'In a few weeks from now I'm meant to be on a married couples panel in the USA to talk about being married.'

I looked up, tears flooding my eyes, and we both burst out laughing. It was just too ludicrous.

'Want a trip to America?' I asked him with resignation. 'Someone's got to come with me.'

Mick said he'd think about it and reassured me that I had a friend in him and that if I needed a shoulder, he had two of them.

Ian and Steve came back to the caravan. Steve looked pale and looked at me with deep feelings. He had been floored by Ian's version of what was happening and had found himself showered with enthusiastic ideas about a new life in a London flat with a sports car writing jingles for TV and had been asked if he thought there would be any TV work back in Canada that Ian might be involved in. Steve felt responsible, afraid that Ian's captivation with him had brought this to the fore. Steve said he was so sorry and brought up the possibility of finishing filming and just doing the best with what they already had. I was insistent. We couldn't stop filming. It was the only structure I had left in my life. I needed something, anything, to continue how it was. Something had to stay the same. He suggested that we not film today and that we all just go somewhere for a change of scene. I agreed. We decided to go down to the sea.

The drive was a cold one, outside and in. Mick and Steve went in one car, Ian and I in another. I piled out of the car as soon as it pulled up, urgent to get away from the source of my confusion and the pain of abandonment. Straight out of the door, I ran down the long winding steps to the beach and the craggy burgundy stretches of rock below, without looking back. I ran, leaping down the steps, trying to let the wind wrap me up and take me somewhere else. I tried to touch the splendour of freedom with the wind. I ran out and out and out across the rocks with the waves rushing over them, tripping over them carelessly like they held no danger. I ran out and out to the very edge of the rocks where I stood over the calling of the tide, deep and green and stretching out for ever. In an instant, I could have jumped into those depths, and so forget my human life and be part of the sea. I could have been encased in its vastness, untouched and unfilthied by the petty effects of a human world that was so transient, a world that could die and could abandon and could change and could reduce my worth to transient material bullshit. By contrast, the wind and the ocean asked for nothing. I had resonated with them all my life. They were within me and through me and for that moment I, too, was one with them. These things could never abandon me and would always be home. The rocks, in the realm of guarantees, stood firm beneath my feet. I looked down at my feet, the waves ebbing to and fro and creating a rhythm, a resonance, a music within me as my soul moved with it in unison and we were together.

The others were approaching, all walking out separately, like stars gathering within a constellation, all heading this way. I looked at them all one by one: Mick who was my warmth, Steve in whom I saw the sadness of my situation reflected so brutally in his empathy, and Ian, so alone and defiant, still looking so childlike, a spited seven-year-old. I understood him too well, too well to hate him for all this, and too well to cast off my empathy and worry about myself.

They had all joined me now, and we stood on the edge of earth on this strange day. We all stood and looked out, watching the sea and its dance. We stood, four people with deep but varying connections, together, empathic and yet solitary, each so solitary. Suddenly, a dolphin sprang out of the water in an arc not far before us out beyond the rocks. It was followed by another, then another, then another. There were four of them. There were four of them and there were four of us. I looked out at them and inside of me I felt grateful. It was a good omen and I knew God or destiny or some guardian angel would not send such a good omen on such a bad day if things were really as bad as they seemed.

I an was in a panic. He had made the decision to go but had no money or place of his own, no job, no social network. With the crew now back at their hotel, like a drowning man he lost no time in trying to secure his future, and there was not a spare moment alone with him in which he was not trying to sort out some loose end, particularly financial.

I just couldn't think on my toes, and Ian with his lightning-speed logic-computer-brain had all the angles. I struggled to respond to each of his requests as best as my small picture brain could. Eventually, I realized he was hounding me and giving me no space to think, no space in which to consider the consequences or wider implications of what I would now agree to.

I refused to talk to him on financial issues without a lawyer. He would say, 'This isn't about money', and I'd believe him. Then he would raise a seemingly new topic, which inevitably rolled back around to money and the ensuing fighting, as I again and again insisted, demanded, I'd not agree to anything financial without a lawyer.

Ian called my accountant, who had by now become something of a friend of ours. In the course of the discussion Ian boldly told him how he felt he had the right to have fifty per cent of everything I had earned. The accountant was shocked and explained calmly to him that he believed that was not a reasonable request. Ian called my literary agent and spoke to his wife, who was a social worker and equally boldly and confidently told her the same. She, too, gave him the same response. The more I or anyone else defied him on this, the more utterly committed he was that he would get 'what he deserved'.

I was a mess. I couldn't handle this. Not only couldn't I handle the intense pressure to respond with no time to think and no legal advice, I also couldn't emotionally bear witness to the absolute boldness with which Ian so clearly and clinically assumed his 'rights'. And I couldn't handle sharing a bed with this man, or a room, or even a house. I had to get some space, some thinking space, some breathing space, some living space. I had already put some things out in the caravan with the feeling it would be easier for me to move than to get Ian to do so in the demanding, defiant and reactive state he was in. I had everything out there that I would need. I moved outside into the caravan.

The crew had left their things out there. They had offered to pack them away, but I had insisted 'no'. Their things gave it a warm feel of connection in the cold, clinical atmosphere of impending disconnection where all security established with Ian seemed for now reduced to who was getting what and how much it cost in pound notes. Here, in the caravan, I was surrounded by things that were detached from this previous social reality, equipment and belongings that belonged to other lives, even Mick's makeshift ashtray on the steps of the caravan outside where the smoke wouldn't affect me. These lives had not hurt me, they were lives that went out there somewhere into the rest of the world, a world of 'the worlders', the world from which Ian had kept me sheltered in our symbiotic insularity.

I listened to the electrical hum of the equipment plugged in to charge and it was as welcome as a cat's purr. I walked among the chaotic jumble of recording equipment, and it gave the warmth of home with its accumulated knick-knacks.

It was late and I went to go to bed. On the dresser in the caravan's bedroom was a stone. I picked it up and found it was two stones, each fitting the other perfectly. I clicked them together and they made the perfect sound. It was clear, I had been left a present. I had second thoughts as to whether Ian was really as inconsiderate as it felt if he had gone out of his way to leave this thoughtful symbol of remembrance.

Mick and Steve arrived at the caravan. I welcomed them into what was now my home, offering them some of their own coffee. It was a warm atmosphere and one of comrades weathering a storm and lending the strength of deeply felt empathy and equality. Mick had a look of empathy so deep I'd have sworn he'd have loaned me his heart for a week if it would have helped.

I saw Ian and said thank you for the stone. He didn't know what I was talking about. He hadn't been out to the caravan. The reprieve of the momentary warmth I had felt suddenly ebbed, subsiding in the moment with the cold reminder not to be such a fool. The stone had not been left by Ian. It had been left by someone else. It had been left by Mick.

Ian progressively dropped out of the filming, asking if he was needed, for if not, he had packing to do as the removals truck would be here in four days.

He had argued that though he'd decided to go, he had nowhere to go. Though he made it clear he'd feel comfortable to stay with the house, there was no way I was leaving my own home. I remembered there was a house bought as an investment which was still waiting to be let. It was a one-bedroom starter home and it was in suburbia about six hours' drive away. Ian wasn't sure. It was a big step down for him and, besides, he couldn't fit all of his things into that small house. He needed something bigger, preferably not terraced or semi-detached where he'd feel threatened and closed in by the proximity of others, preferably with a garden and parking and somewhere quiet.

I had received advice about legal avenues by now. In a formal tone of finality, I let him know he had till the end of the day to decide if he was sure and then I'd call in a legal conciliator who'd negotiate the issues on my behalf. By the end of the day, he had conceded that he'd tolerate this one-bedroom house until something else was organized. That something else was that I would buy him a larger house of his choosing.

Ian made it clear he had nothing to live on, or money with which to buy appliances for the new home. Doing a few hours' work each week around the house and as my PA, he'd been living off my income for the past two and a half years since he'd quit his job, with credit cards and free access to the accounts which I'd had put into joint names. Without a lawyer, and in order to be rid of his harassment, I agreed to give him a lump sum of ten thousand pounds for anything he'd need to buy, agreed he could take almost all the household goods, rent-free use of the investment property he was going to and that I would pay him a weekly salary for a year. He felt this would do until the property settlement went through in which he had every intention to go for what he saw as 'his legal entitlement'.

He brought up the issue of a car. When we had met I had no car and hadn't needed one. When I bought one it was unroadworthy and couldn't be driven. I sold it for less than a thousand pounds, and Ian, too, had sold his own car for about the same. In their place, I paid for a Mercedes. Ian had researched it, and though it had cost a load of money, my money sense at the time meant there wasn't too much difference between two thousand pounds and twenty thousand pounds. It was said to be about the safest and cleanest car there was, and Ian, who was the driver, felt safe and good driving it. The registration document required only one name. As we now faced having to sell the car, I now found out that the car had never been in my name. The car dealership had taken Ian's name. It was decided the car would be sold to a dealership for a quick price and the money split so Ian could buy a car and I'd still have one myself.

The crew and I filmed mostly outside. Sometimes tears would run down my face as I spoke and we'd take a break and then start again. As we filmed, Ian drove back and forth getting boxes for his packing. In the two and a half years we'd been together, he had always wanted me to be with him if leaving the property or if anyone visited. When I had wanted to leave, it had always been clear that he would come with me. Now, finally now, and in these severing circumstances, Ian no longer insisted on being accompanied, or on accompanying me.

Steve needed to do some filming indoors so filmed in the caravan. Sometimes we needed to film in the house. Steve, Mick and I all went in like visitors and would find a place where the boxes weren't in the background of the shot.

The house was empty and alien. I just wanted to leave with the crew. I didn't want to be here when they left. I wanted to leave with them out into the world. Not alone here on this big empty farm with big empty rooms and the spectre of abandonment for company.

There were just two days of filming left and then the crew would leave. Steve had to do some arranging of a scene at a local butterfly farm. He and Mick climbed into the car.

I stood watching them leave from about thirty feet away. Suddenly, I felt great dread. In two and a half years I hadn't spent a single day on my own. I hadn't driven a car on my own or caught public transport on my own or gone shopping on my own or even visited a neighbour's house on my own, or even seen anybody socially on my own. I had never even been in someone else's car without Ian in the last two and a half years. Ian had spent every single day with me.

As Steve started up the car, I knew they were my last chance of surviving what would surely be a powerful grip of agoraphobia once Ian left. I'd been agoraphobic once before and for me it was just an extension of the Exposure Anxiety I'd fought all my life and to which I was still highly susceptible.

My body was gripped with tremors as I stepped towards the car.

'Please,' I said as I became overcome completely with tears. 'I have to come with you. If I don't learn now to go out without Ian, I'm really scared I won't be able to get out of this property.'

They understood. I climbed in and we drove away, leaving Ian, on his own, at the property.

At the beach we stopped. Now only three of us. Steve dropped off me and Mick and drove on to the butterfly farm alone.

We sat on the grass for a while and we laughed and I cried. We went walking down on the rocks. His company was easy, like a warm breeze. There was no insecurity, no clinging. His smile warmed me, and my smile warmed him, and the sun shone down on both of us. It was Simply Be.

We sat on the rocks. This was the first time Mick had seen me outside of the context of Ian's wife, here, just us, on the beach. We could see each other: Donna who was just Donna and Mick who was who he was when not being just part of the film crew.

Steve returned and we went to a cafe. Steve ordered a hot chocolate that I couldn't have because of dairy intolerance and food allergies. Mick ordered a sausage roll that I couldn't have either. I ordered a mineral water, and just to be fancy I gave myself four straws, each a different colour and poked them into the bottle. We all laughed.

As we returned to the farm there was a sad air hovering. These people, my friends, felt deeply for me but they were leaving tomorrow. As glad as I knew they would be to get back to their own lives, I knew it would hurt them to go. I had seen the deepest of empathy in their eyes. I had felt love from them and deep understanding and admiration for my strength. I had felt a caring from them wrap around me and I knew their thoughts were with me, and that had mattered to me a lot. But I cared, also, very deeply for them. I wanted them not to worry and I wanted them to be free. I wrote them a note.

*Hello,*

*You people will go some time tomorrow. In whatever way you became woven into the chaos here, nobody caused any of the chaos and change – however like eating shit it may be, it is sometimes just a street that branches off or turns sharply – some roads rough or full of potholes, the streets dark and hard to see down, but life is not lived on the grass verge even if you curse that road for moving under your feet or looking daunting.*

*I want to tell you people – feel bad for nothing – your presence didn't bring the change, you just stepped into our lives whilst the road under our feet took off with lightning speed. (Speaking from my side only) You people became my safe place here as the safe place of predictability had a face lift. You made a temporary bridge here and I do feel strong in my self containment, so don't worry. Also, I have a good network of trustable people – even if it is their paid job. I just have to dig them back out of the woodwork. I have a few trusted unpaid people too. My goal is to get off this escalator when I meet the fork in the road with my name on it – and I'll know it when I do. It will be signposted 'peace this way'. Until then, knowing I can speak with either of you people is a big security in my pocket. I won't feel guilty to have laughed or joked or enjoyed company in this big drama – those were the breaks in the clouds where I saw ME with awareness – (that sounds like a good signpost to me – these shoes fit). I distinguish between selfish and self.*

*Anyway, in a nutshell – thank you and don't worry – seriously. I say this not emptily in order to appease or out of fear – I say it because I feel things will work out in their own way. It is hard to know if the balance of give and take fell heavy on my side. It's easier when you pay people. Some people have just liked to know me and I understand they feel that is life not badly spent. I think company was enjoyed here so I figure that I probably don't owe.*

*With very good feelings,*

*From Donna*

The sun came up on the day of goodbye. The air was clean and bright and uplifting. I cooked breakfast on the caravan stove and looked out on the sheep out in the field. The crew would leave today, and Ian would leave only three days later. His removal truck was booked. His packing was done. I had no idea at all what sort of life I was headed for but somehow, nothing felt wrong.

The crew showed up and I made them welcome in the caravan. Ian went about his arrangements inside the big, progressively emptying house, in there with the telephone and the fancy cooker, the central heating and the wall-to-wall carpet.

He asked us all to lunch. He was making soup. We all accepted and dined out on the front lawn, each of us somehow facing outwards further into the field and not looking at each other.

Ian ran through ideas of what sort of car he would buy and had figured on a sports car that would only have two doors and no space for passengers. He spoke of his ideas for employment and courses he might do.

I spoke of the job of finding homes for all the animals: a Shetland pony, two Vietnamese pigs and the two sheep. I spoke of the possibility of moving back to Australia, and of getting someone in to share the house and of selling it and starting again somewhere else.

Evening was approaching. Steve and Mick had a long drive ahead of them. The four of us got up from the lawn and walked towards the gate. We all stopped and faced each other. We were standing in a circle, Steve opposite Ian, Mick opposite me. There was an energy present as we all stood silent.

'I think some magic happened here,' I said out loud.

The crew packed the car and climbed in. Ian had returned to the house.

'I'll hear from you soon,' said Mick through the car window.

I ran my finger over the car bonnet and caught the dew, tossing it into the air. Then they drove away.

It took only ten days between Ian's announcement and his leaving. After the crew left, we went through the house making an inventory of what he would pack and what he would put in storage and how much money he would need to set up a life elsewhere. The car would be sold and the money for it split between us so we were each mobile.

On his last day in the house, I moved in from outside. The bed had been disassembled for the van the next day and he had set up the airbed to sleep on. I was welcomed into the house and he offered me to sleep next to him on the airbed which had been made up on the floor of what was now the empty lounge room. I came in from the caravan and brought my things in. He cooked dinner for us both, we watched the TV that would stay and later lay down to sleep. We lay up against each other like in the early days. We smelled each other's hair and felt the contours of each other's faces. We linked fingers and did butterfly hands and our faces were moist from tears, though we each cried for and to ourselves for the impending leaving neither of us fully understood.

Ian's delivery van arrived the next morning and took him and his many many boxes across to the other side of the country. After it left, I stood in what now seemed an empty and deserted house. There was no bed, no lounge suite. I went on a tour through the abandoned upstairs rooms. The long spacious room which had once been the bedroom now seemed something of a joke, with a solitary wardrobe standing in one corner – my corner. The other upstairs room had been Ian's hobby room and was now totally empty. Downstairs, the lounge room looked just as strange, a single bookcase standing in an otherwise empty room. Ironically, only my office area seemed to have any lived-in feel to it.

Just before Ian left, he had come with me to buy a bed, a single bed. And I had bought a sofa, a small sofa to sit in front of the television in the huge house for one.

The bed now arrived and I decided not to take it upstairs at all. I moved it into the only room that felt familiar – the office. I had bought a duvet cover and curtains and put them up. They were tartan, the pattern which had always carried the feel of my grandmother. I would symbolically bring her back through the tartan. That was what I needed now. I needed to feel enveloped within whatever remnants of a sense of home I could find. The paintings and pictures that were left I spread out throughout the house to make it not so bare. I put up three I liked most in what was now the new bedroom.

Ian hadn't had time to move any of the remaining furniture for me and I was in no mood or state for company, or for the asking of help. What would be my wardrobe was upstairs. I merely tumbled the big lug of a thing out into the hall and slid it down the stairs, hoping it wouldn't gouge the walls too much and would arrive at the bottom in one piece and useable.

As night fell in the shell that had once been a home, the loneliness of the unlit countryside closed in. Surrounded by acres of uninhabited green, without a neighbour within even shouting distance, I felt small, very small, in this foreign country.

A package arrived in the postbox. It was a photo of my father, dead in his coffin, thin, grey and gaunt like a skeleton of who he once had been now dressed in his business suit with one of the roses I'd sent held in his hand and lying in his arm. It came with a letter from my mother saying she'd taken this photo just in case I wanted to have a little funeral for him of my own in which I could burn his photo. The photo reminded me of the look of my grandfather when, as a child, I had found him dead, his face half purple from a massive heart attack.

I felt very very vulnerable, especially with my mother's words and deeds sent ten thousand miles across the sea and still here in my hands. I felt gripped with dread. What had happened to the poetry book I had sent Jackie Paper? Had she seen the poem about him? Did she know I had disclosed to the whole world what had happened to him?

They had had the will changed back into their favour in the last two weeks of Jackie Paper's life and divided all he had, but had sent in this package three sets of cufflinks and a watch. I remembered the cufflinks and staring into the red stones getting lost in the colour till I was blissed. I remembered the ones with the little paintings on, paintings cohesive simply because being so tiny they didn't fragment like most things did. I remembered the Christmas he tried to give me the watch. It was years ago, the year I left for the UK. He had bought my mother a T-shirt and had a watch for me. He had been instructed to give me her T-shirt because I wouldn't want 'that gaudy thing' which was the watch. I had said nothing and simply took the T-shirt he had intended for her. I had never seen that watch again till now. So finally, I had got it. I put it on, and surprisingly it worked. The tiny rhinestones around the watch face caught the light as I walked back up the driveway. I tore up the letter but felt unable to tear up a picture of my father, even one so tragic and confusing as this one. I put it in the photo album next to the one of him smiling and alive and took the cufflinks to put into my box of special things. Then I played the piano, coming out with a song that was beautiful and moving and called it 'Is He Home?'

> I wonder if he's home tonight,
> He's always on my mind when I'm alone.
> I don't know why, why it always seems to be
> That something stops me reaching for the phone.
> And here I sit a world away.
> Is it pride or is it fear? Well I don't know.
> If he were here, he wouldn't make me stay
> Would try to stop me if I went to go.
> I wonder if he's home tonight.
> If I wanted just to see him and if I really didn't need him,
> It wouldn't hurt so much for me to call.
> It wouldn't hurt so much, so much at all.

It was strange in the big empty house and easy, too easy for the child in me to think of this five-hundred-year-old place as haunted. I wanted to run but there was nowhere to run to. There was no place for me. I'd been away from Australia for so long there was no place for me back there, and I needed to be here, to keep myself safe.

For three years, I had responded and adjusted to Ian's presence and now I had to think for myself, without prompt. It taught me a lot about susceptibility to laziness and passivity. I had never seen myself that way, yet when someone else reinforces daily that you can't or shouldn't do things for yourself, and does so in the name of caring, it's amazing how much more mindless you can become. I knew how some old people simply rusted up in the hands of carers and how some special needs kids were kept wrapped in this sort of unquestionable cotton wool swaddling from so early on they would never imagine or question that they may in fact be far more capable than this. At least I had the memory that, however klutzy I was in organizing information, I had been a fiercely independent child, leaving by the window and off to the park at the age of three. I had found myself a new family and thrown rocks at my friend's window to be let in when I was eight. I had taken off with the first stranger who suggested it at the age of fifteen, and in spite of homelessness, poverty and lack of education, had taken myself back to school and beyond. Short-sighted, naïve in spite of a wealth of experience, with learning difficulties, you bet. But if nothing else, I was one of the most determined and resilient and adaptable people I'd ever known.

It was hard to go out. For me things ticked when I didn't think. Everything got stilted and jumbled when I tried to be conscious of what I was doing. That's when the self-protection responses would fire and wreak havoc. Left to bimble along, pretty much things would work out in the end.

Now I got a map and found out how to get to the town I had been to every week for two years. Out of touch with my capacity simply to map out the feel of how to get there, I started the car, drove down the road and got lost less that fifteen minutes from the house.

Finally, I made it to the shops with my shopping list, parked the car and went to buy some whiteboards to write on, oh, and a new wedding ring. I would never hold it together unless I could keep track of one day to the next, and the ring was to be able to throw away the wedding ring I bought myself when marrying Ian, so I could still wear one but one which had no association with that time, a kind of marriage to myself. It would also be a way of avoiding questions and fending off any other interested party. Then I needed … Oh shit, the parking ticket. I didn't have one. I ran back to the car, got there and couldn't remember why I was back. Had I left something in the car? Did I want to drop off the whiteboards? I looked at my note. I hadn't finished my shopping. I put the whiteboards in the car and left again.

Back home I didn't feel like talking to anyone. I felt like it was somehow labelled on me that I was something left behind, abandoned, some sort of food scrap scraped off the side of the plate because it had gone off, was distasteful or had become boring. I didn't want to be asked why I was alone when my partner had always been seen with me. The phone kept ringing, and without Ian there to filter, all the calls were picked up by the answer machine. Faxes kept coming in and piled onto the floor. Papers came through the post and I opened them. I wanted to keep up with things. I didn't need any chaos from unpaid bills or things I had overlooked. I just needed to clear the cotton wool out of my head and hold all the pieces together without my confetti thoughts drifting like a million mini kites without strings.

Brebis and Schaf said maa-aa out in the field. In all the catastrophe they were missing attention. I went and spent time with them. Brebis came up to me as usual, craving attention and wagging her little cropped stub of a tail like a big chunky dog glad to see me. Schaf, who'd been taken care of mostly by Ian, seemed to have sensed something wrong and was becoming more aloof. I simply wasn't Ian and never would be. I wasn't her 'maa-aa'. All she had was her sister, Brebis. She was turning her back on the world of humans.

Each day consisted of get up, get washed, get dressed, have breakfast, fetch the post, which with all the involuntary avoidance, diversion and retaliation responses now took at least half of the day. The rest was spent writing and composing in this hollow shell of a house with its loud ticking clock, and I wrote:

*The clock keeps time on the wall*
*As a spider spins up a web like a net there to catch me as I fall.*
*And the sound of myself as I breathe,*
*Fills the room like music forgotten,*
*Boxed up with the lies that we believed.*
*This picture sits in the frame with a smile,*
*By the phone so alone, like a fashion that faded out of style,*
*And the coat on the peg by the door is like a notice,*
*Pinned up, left behind, by the ghosts that don't live here anymore.*
*I'm making up my mind, I'm wasting no more time*
*Chasing old memories of yesterday.*
*I'm making up my mind, I'm wasting no more time chasing shadows,*
*The shadows of who we were, and shadows of you,*
*The shadows of what we once knew.*

I opened the painted glass door to the bread oven which served as the letter box at the end of the drive, the mock stained-glass parrots stenciled on there and painted by Ian. Among the bundle of letters was one from a fan telling me I was a reincarnated dolphin spirit. Thank you very much.

Another was from the Allergy-Induced Autism Support Group. I had called them ages ago, having had their number for over a year before I finally got around to it. I had forgotten about them.

The letter was an information pack and contained various articles relating to phenol intolerance. I had been diagnosed by two allergy clinics as being severely allergic to phenol and salicylate, and I thought that as I didn't eat stone fruits and strawberries I was pretty much sorted. Suddenly, a list jumped out at me from the information pack. It was an exhaustive list of the foods rich in various types of phenols. The article also listed which allergy-related conditions the different phenols were associated with. Jumping out among the list which included migraine, arthritis and asthma, were epilepsy, hyperactivity, dyslexia, and autism. I took hold of the reins of diet and tightened them.

I had been on a diet for seven years, a diet free of all milk products, free of sugar and all additives and mostly free of wheat. For a while I'd also been off grapes, tomatoes, strawberries, cherries, plums and berries, all of which either caused muscle constriction or made me clearly manic, hyper and 'drunk'. But I'd lost the list and forgotten what was on it and what was not, and so much had crept back in. I had had bread perhaps ten times in seven years and hadn't had shop-bought sweet biscuits, lasagne, pizza, chocolate, or any of the other things I had so much binged on but which gave me dark puffy rings under my eyes, arthritis, asthma, recurrent ear and chest infections and, of course, utterly did my head in.

Throughout childhood and up until seven years ago, I'd had all sorts of addictive food binges. Jars of honey eaten by the spoonful, cane sugar syrup drunk straight out of the tin, blocks of cheese consumed as a lunch, whole lemons and chocolate cake breakfasts. I would sit in cafes and eat the sugar cubes compulsively, tip the sugar bowl up and fill my mouth with the granules like sand into a quarry. I ate whole bunches of celery, lettuce and cucumber, lived furiously on tomato paste and pastas and had been on diets of mashed apple, or 'potato diets' where I would eat nothing else for a few weeks. Grapes couldn't be kept away from me, and if I ate one, the whole bunch went down. Strawberries and cherries, apricots and plums had been the same. If I was 'off my face' and 'in another world', well, that was just Donna.

That had started changing seven years ago. The food binges stopped and I began to lose a grip on what had been 'my world' whether I liked it or not. I was no longer oblivious to sensation and couldn't tune it out.

My moods were more stable and my comprehension more consistent, my sensory buzzing not so manically high and not so often.

My moods were still all over the place, but a vast improvement on seven years ago. I still had panic attacks, sensory-perceptual shutdowns where meaning fell out of what I saw, heard or felt, and occasional compulsive and involuntary tic-like urges to self-abuse. I still had minor states of 'big black nothingness' and severe reactive hypoglycemia with its associated cold extremities, dizzy spells, highs, acute anxiety and epilepsy-like fade-outs were still my daily comrade. But all these things were less severe and less frequent and the daily regime of nutritional supplements seemed to keep me afloat.

There was no doubt I was doing better than I ever had been. My father had died, my husband had left, and I was still holding it reasonably together, albeit living by the instructions on a whiteboard and newly written notes up in every room telling me the structure of the day from breakfast and vitamins, through washing and dressing to reading the post. Nevertheless, just about everything I had been eating was on this list.

I opened the fridge door to look for something to eat. Damn, not a thing in there that wasn't on this doctor's list of the foods. Had my diet really slipped that badly?

I went to the health food store, the grocer's and the butcher's and got everything which wasn't on the list. Then I cleaned out the cupboards at home and piled everything suspect into a box and took it to the house of the farmer who'd given us the sheep. Then I went home for dinner.

It could well have been the effect of Ian being gone, but three days on the strict low-salicylate diet again and I found I didn't need to follow my lists. I started holding it just fine in my head. I started to think with the thoughts not drifting quickly out of reach of conscious grasp. I began to respond to physical and emotional sensations without it even occurring to me that some niggle of unknown form or purpose had gripped me. I felt a consistent clarity I hadn't had and wondered what had happened in my life that my thinking and feeling had changed so fast in so few days. I began to think about contacting people, about building contacts and finding things to do and places to go.

Maybe it was like shock to my system but it was like someone changed the cotton wool in my head for a brain. It was like my mind had just woken up. I had always needed to see my thoughts through writing, or represented and played out through objects in order to hold them coherently. Now, suddenly, I was finding myself thinking in my head. It wasn't the insular thinking that happens when the world feels external, detached, alien, irrelevant or miles away. It was a sort of integral thinking that didn't objectify the world beyond me, I was thinking within the context of that world and about my current place in it. It was happening in bursts, like grabbing a view through a window before the curtains keep getting drawn, but it was a view nevertheless.

I sat in the field and Brebis came trotting over in her great rounded woolliness pushing me over and trying to sit on me. She was simply too big these days and too heavy, but inside her she was just a lamb wanting the closeness of a lamb. I sat quite a while in the field, letting the day tick by.

In a week I was due to speak in the USA as a guest speaker before around six hundred people. Ian and I were to have been on a married couples panel along with other married people with autism and were going to speak about autistic marriage. This upcoming trip would not be any more jolting than the present day-to-day reality I'd run headlong into, so I decided I'd still attend the conference and I'd still speak.

I needed someone to travel with me. I'd always travelled with Ian and I didn't yet trust to travel on my own as I had a tendency to mix up check-in times and gate numbers, and often didn't recognize what the announcements were saying even if they called out my name. I had asked Mick, who said he'd think about it.

'Hello,' said Mick in his stored one-size-fits-all tone as he picked up the phone.

'Hi,' I replied in a peep, my heart thumping with the daring of having called. 'I'm coming up Newcastle way. Want to meet?'

I heard Mick take a drag on his cigarette and a sip of his coffee. Then he agreed to meet me at my hotel.

I drove in a world of my own wrapped up warm in the feel of Mick's company. I was excited like an orphan heading for adoption.

The door to my tiny hotel room sounded with a gentle knock and my heart leaped. I answered and Mick stood there smiling, looking from my face to his shoes and back again. I invited him in.

'Got any coffee?' asked Mick.

'Yep,' I replied trying to coordinate the kettle, the cups and the coffee like a three-ring circus.

We went out and walked through the park together, and Mick wondered why in all his time in Newcastle he hadn't thought to do so before. I picked up a broken shard of plastic, a piece of someone's broken tail light and looked at Mick in a red world. We walked on, and I sensed the feel of him mapped out through my body as I resonated with his energy. He picked up a feather and handed it to me in silence without looking. I smoothed it out and tickled it upon my arm as we walked along.

On the way back to the hotel, I beckoned Mick to follow and headed for a hefty pile of autumn leaves, running into them, tossing a pile high above me and then spinning into the beautiful shower that fell over us both.

Back at the hotel, Mick sat on the floor and I sat up on the single bed. A funny shy smile came over his face and he blurted: 'About America. I've decided. I'm going.'

For the six hours it took to get back to the house my chest felt filled with twittering little birds. He was everything I remembered, his company so warm and easy I could slip into it like a big snuggy old chair. If he had a sign on him saying 'good home', I would have thrown myself in that direction saying 'take me'. But he belonged to an aloof world of Jack the Lad, pubs and clubs and 'I'll let you know' and 'Yeah, that'd be nice, mate'. He had the unspoken words 'noncommital' blazoned across his forehead in neon lights. These feelings of mine were too strong for the words 'little sister'.

I met Mick at the train station, where we'd agreed to meet at the shop that had Paddington Bear. Mick stubbed out a cigarette and stifled the smile his cheeks were full of. His shoulders rounded around his stocky body, he looked far more huggy than Paddington any day. He gave a little wave and we walked together to catch the train to Heathrow. At the airport we collected our tickets like a pair of kids headed for Disneyland. It was time to board the plane to the USA. I ate up his company like a kid gorging itself on chocolate for the soul.

He was easy company. As easy as a breeze. We joked about lightly, played backgammon, which Ian had taught me over three years, and chattered about the events of the last few weeks and what the USA would be like in Indiana.

Mick had never been to the USA at all. I talked him a picture of what it would be like. It was a small-town place we were going to in middle America with its doll's house villages, in one of which we had a hired holiday home awaiting.

The plane arrived and we were met by a sign-bearing woman associated with the conference I'd come to speak at. We followed her to the house in a hire car, Mick driving, me laid back and listening to the familiar tape that he had sent me.

The woman fussed as little as someone excited and instructed not to fuss could manage and then left us to it. Mick and I explored the house. It was a little grandma house surrounded by forestry with a front porch made for a rocking chair, a little shared bathroom and an all in one kitchenette, dining area and lounge room. There was one bedroom. That would be mine. Mick had the sofa out in the lounge room.

A collection of jigsaws had been left for us, and Mick had discovered cable TV. He sat for a moment flicking through US channels, amused by the hoo-ha these people spent time absorbed in.

I went outside to feel the trees. It was dark, and I felt the dew of the grass under my feet. I sat there in the cleansing silent acceptance of nature for a while, then came back in.

It wasn't easy to talk to Mick now that I was so consciously aware we would actually be sharing a house for ten days. I went for the jigsaw. He joined me.

At night I got into my sleeping clothes and put my recently acquired friend, Travel Bear, into bed. I said goodnight to Mick, looking at him and was glad he had come.

The next morning, I got up at dawn and went out among the trees in the dawn light, treading softly past Mick's slumbering mass. He looked like an angel, and I'm sure he was. I wanted to touch his hair. I wanted just to touch his arm. I...

Back inside, the angel still slept, snoring away, oblivious in sleep as I'd been in life. I went into my bedroom and listened to some music. I was bursting with the feeling of 'social' and I typed a letter to my friend in the next room.

*Good Morning, Mick.*

*Everything is changing, so fast it is really hard to keep up with. This morning I heard a song on the Walkman that I don't know and I could keep up with every single word sung WITH MEANING as each one happened. It scared me A LOT. I often know songs off by heart but I learn words as strings of sound and analyse them for meaning afterwards, so the joining together of words and music for feeling doesn't usually happen together – unless they're my songs. This was weird, sort of like the guts of the song jumped out with meaning and feeling. Welcome to the world – I always wonder when these sudden 'wake ups' are going to stop. Each time these big steps happen, I have to re-assess 'I' – i.e.: isn't 'I' the person who just heard these things as strings of sounds and gets them with effort long after the moment is passed? I'm keeping up with the moment – the world just might be more than Postman Pat after all.*

*Then, I had big feelings about my father being gone and they were too big but I let sadness happen for ten minutes and the fear of big emotion didn't cause me to shut it out – well at least for ten minutes but by then sadness was escalating to panic so it was probably a good idea – but ten minutes is A BIG GLIMPSE of big feelings about another person. Feelings about myself or my own life aren't so bad to handle – you know where they stop and start because it's your own life – somewhere there are answers. Feelings for another person are different. You can't control where they begin and end – especially, maybe, if that person is gone.*

*Other things – I'm asking people about themselves – you, my publisher – just something I'm finding in me. But it's not the fact-collecting thing like before and it's not just 'buzz food'. It's strange to find this in me. It requires all these mechanics that weren't there just a few weeks ago – the ability to strongly hold thought that comes from feeling without it drifting away with a lightning-quick mental 'oops' that erases it like a mistake on a blackboard before a person even gets to read what was there (probably partly complements of my enemy anxiety). Anyway, what else is so hard to emotionally/mentally deal with is the awareness that comes with this that this is what everyone else has – if I have this too, then I'm getting more like them – but I hope I will never become a 'the worlder' (as in the narrow-minded, arrogant, prejudiced and ignorant crap sense of the word). I think not though, I think I'd have a long way to go to be that and I don't think my map is taking me there because there's nothing that rotten in my soul or I'd think I'd have had a whiff of the stench by now and I wouldn't be my friend so much as I am.*

*Well, there is no point to this letter. Just a sharing – another cloud breaks and the sunshine breaks through (I actually have a piece of music called Sunshine Through Clouds). A pointless letter with no real reason to write it seems a nice thing I think.*

*I just found a point – oh well. I wanted to let you know that if I seem quiet in a bit of a sad or reflective way sometimes (without being in my own world), there is nothing you have done to upset me AT ALL – it's just that sometimes it takes time to get to know the shoes you find yourself in – what's nice is these seem to fit better all the time. What a life.*

*Donna*

Jean had flown down here to Indiana from upstate to be with me. She was a journalist who had become a friend over the past six years, but spent the last two to three years cut off from me as Ian filtered all her calls. She was down staying with a friend and would join me at the conference for support in Ian's absence. Mick liked her on sight and she warmed to him, and the two of them shared coffee in common. We were also invited to dinner at the log cabin that she and her friend had rented.

Mick was seeing me outside of the context of filming and Wales and he seemed fascinated and pleasantly surprised by the extent to which he enjoyed my company. I would find him just watching me, a peaceful, rather beautiful calm on his face that looked like deep empathy. Then, caught, he would look away as if caught up in a warm blanket he gave himself. I felt happy just that he was happy. I found it difficult to look back. I felt I would be affected by it and didn't know where that would take me. I was happy where things were. I knew how to cope with this. Anything bigger was beyond me right now, a chocolate bar too big for my face.

It had been two days now. With the help of a new smart drug, an amino acid called Glutamine, I had held it together with consistency, able to experience Mick and me simultaneously, never losing meaning in any major sensory drop-out. We shared the cooking, we sat out on the porch together and watched the fire together. If someone could have woven me a fairytale it was this. I felt this must be what others call 'normal'.

I dragged Mick from shop to shop, exploring Christmas decorations and exotic worlds within glass paperweights, tickled squealingly by kitsch advertisements and gimmicks, and walking along in the remnants of sunshine left from a season on its way out.

Back at the house, Mick, a stocky cheeky-faced man with dancing eyes wrapped up in a soul which buttoned it down like a tight jacket so that it all seemed to pop out the seams, had out a tub of ice-cream. The ice-cream was made from rice milk and didn't have dairy products or sugar, but I knew it had berries and grape concentrate: things that weren't on my OK list. But to share ice-cream with this man, to have eaten from the same spoon, was like an invitation to the Cinderella ball from the prince himself. And who was I to let the ugly sisters hold me back? Mick was feeling guilty as he tucked into it. He offered a spoonful saying: 'I guess you can't have any of this.'

In spite of knowing I had addictive craving for berries and grapes and got 'drunk' on them, I went for the spoon. A tiny bit wouldn't hurt. We headed off to Jean's log cabin just fifteen minutes away.

On the way we stopped at a place to fill the car with fuel. Theoretically, all the understanding was there but none of it connected with experience. But fifteen minutes the other side of the ice-cream, I had a brain full of lint and nothing made sense. Perhaps it was epilepsy, for I had been tested for it in my twenties after having fugues and was told I had atypical epilepsy. It could have been that certain chemical highs triggered this mind-blanking state and that it was nothing to do with the ice-cream. Whatever it was, I knew who Mick was theoretically, but the understood concept of him had left and all that was left was a 3-D animated Mick impression. I watched the man move about with a long petrol hose and felt anxious and out of control. Mick asked if I was OK. It meant nothing. Just sounds. Sounds of nothing from what had once been a friend who was now just an animated impression. I didn't want to be here. I couldn't stand to lose the grip on experienced interpretative meaning that I had just come to accept could be mine, the heaven of social sharing. Now, brutally, I was again plunged straight back into a world of one and I hated and I feared, and I wanted out. And there was nothing and nowhere and no-one.

I wandered off. The sound of gravel under my feet was a familiar sound to me, an old friend. I picked some up and hit the pieces together with the wordless feeling of 'I know you'. I had found a spark of hope.

I hated the abandonment of being thrown out of cohesion and belonging. I resented that no-one stopped it, because I certainly couldn't. I felt shamed to have known this world, this beautiful world so wholly, so fully, and held it with consistency. And what the hell for? To lose it with the spiteful striking reminder of life itself that this newly found experienced reality was not mine no matter how much I valued it.

In silence, I walked back to Mick tapping the stones. I recalled how the impression that was now him had once made sounds with the rocks, made them for me to hear, to share them and meet me in what was 'my world', this stinking shithole of a realm back into which I'd just been plunged against my will. I tapped the stones together, staring at him with asking eyes. He looked back with reaching eyes that held understanding and sadness.

I climbed into the car like a child which had soiled itself, tapping my stones and triggering the remembrance of the words associated with the sound, saying 'rocks', 'rocks', 'rocks' to myself.

'Rocks?' I said, half a question, half a statement.

'Rocks,' replied Mick, continuing to drive to Jean's house.

The climax of meaning loss had been reached and it had started to trickle back in. I got anxious and agitated as we turned into the street for Jean's cabin. I signed to stop. Mick stopped the car. I unbuckled my belt and turned in my seat, holding the back of the chair and crying. I felt such unbearable shame. I was heading to see my friend and couldn't thoroughly hold the slippery concept. She'd see me but see me like this. She'd see me shamed and helpless and out of it, reduced more to an animal in my processing than a person. Mick waited as I cried.

'Are you ready?' he asked as I started to talk with some fluency.

I nodded.

We arrived at Jean's log cabin armed with user-friendly food from my short little list. Jean answered the door, took one look at me, realized we had a crisis and said 'Hi Mick', and led him out into the kitchen to where her friend Johnny was.

Jean returned to me just inside the door. She knew what had happened. We sat and I cried it out of me, telling her how ashamed I was to lose it, how bitterly cruel it was for life to let me hold cohesion and then rob it in a glimpse.

'It will come back,' she reassured.

I knew she was right. I knew it was just an acute allergic reaction or epilepsy and that now I wasn't living day to day, meal to meal on such foods I would get it back, even if I was now a prisoner of diet, someone with a dietary disability who could function only with the use of a dietary wheelchair. It just seemed so bloody unfair. Here I was having wanted cohesive multitrack processing more than anything in the world and now the stakes had gone up. Now I'd had it, I was angry at having to stay on the diet that was my only way of holding it.

The rest of the evening went great after dinner. I was with the land of the living again and kept up as the conversation shifted from Jean and Johnny, to Jean and Mick, to Mick and me, to me and Jean. I wasn't external or a world away. My own conversation was on the same track and flowed with theirs, not going off on my own tangent, oblivious to whether it matched their topic or not. I caught Mick looking at me with warmth, with belonging, with pride. I caught Jean looking from Mick to me with a smile. I caught Johnny being full of himself and oblivious to the rest of us, but funny as he kept us all entertained while he and Mick shared wine. I caught me feeling what 'home' was and wishing that somewhere in my life one day I'd have this forever.

The next day, Jean, Mick and I all arrived at the conference, and our little team was escorted into a quiet room to wait for my turn to speak. I was connected up and multitrack and was scared to order a meal, but I knew that if I didn't eat before talking, the anxiety from talking would create havoc. I ordered some food I felt sure I could eat safely and prayed silently to myself not to let it do my head in before going out there to speak in front of six hundred people who'd paid and travelled to hear and see me.

It was time for me to speak. The three of us walked to the room and I walked up the front to the married couples panel. They had agreed for me to give an opening address to the panel rather than be part of it, considering my partner couldn't be there. I stood at the microphone with six hundred eyes on me, none of them knowing that the person about to talk about an autistic marriage had just experienced not the finding of it but its loss.

Another autistic woman, Kathy, sprawled out along the table where the couples sat, her husband next to her. She beamed her sunny Midwestern smile at me and looked at me with simple adoration. Another woman with autism came forward out of the audience with a camera and signed sharply to me to sit down. I obeyed and she took the photo, handing me a sketch she had done of me from across the room. A man from across the room looked at me with a startling depth. I looked back and he crossed the room, introducing himself with 'Thank you, you saved my life'. A folded note was passed to me from another person with autism. It read 'I love you, I love you, I love you' over and over again. These people felt I was their people. They looked to me with belonging, with hope and for direction. I was merely the teller of my own tales. What had I given them?

I looked at the faces who had come to hear about marriage and autism. I started to speak.

'Many people believe that people with autism can't form relationships. Well, I'm a third generation married person with autism.'

The way I saw it, autism was just normality with the volume turned way way up. Though there are elements of autism in many people, there were, in my personal opinion, definite elements of this high volume in my father who was, at the least, dyslexic, manic and compulsive, with a few rather Autie traits. My father's mother lived in her own world and would probably these days have been called 'able autistic'. Two cousins on my father's side of the family had been diagnosed with Asperger Syndrome, two others had Crohn's Disease and another with Coeliac Disease. For what it was worth, I considered myself third generation.

I talked of my grandmother as a woman passed from one relationship to the next, accumulating children and dying alone, predominantly more in her own little world than in the world. I talked of the relationship between my father and my mother; one the child in the adult's body, utterly without shame, the other brutally and excruciatingly aware of imperfection and an adult who I felt had never been a child.

Finally, I talked of my own marriage, so reflective of that of my own parents. I talked of the logical Asperger frustrated by the processing problems of the autistic, yet moved by the sensuality which came with inconsistent meaning. I talked of the autistic feeling constant pressure to keep up with the quick, calculating and logical mind that was the more left-brain dominant home of the Asperger. I talked of acceptance of difference but still being equal, of the system of 'simply being' and of understanding in an often ignorant world. And only once did I make the mistake of using past tense in referring to my marriage. At the end, many people were crying and I no longer felt guilty for I knew I hadn't hurt their feelings, I had moved them. As an act of respect, the audience stood in silence and it was the best thank you they could have given me.

Out of the talk, my body quaked with the adrenaline rush of finally letting go. I was gripped with wild and manic movements as I sought to shake the impulses out of me.

'What do you need?' asked Mick.

'Jump,' I spluttered.

Mick moved out of the way and I jumped on the bed back in the room the staff had set aside for me to wind down. I jumped and I squealed and I cried. Then I made a bee-line for the shower and turned the water on myself, clothes and all.

Mick and I drove back to the cabin, him driving, me lying back on the car seat with the sound of our special music playing. He was a real-life Travel Bear and I knew he'd be a friend for always, if only in my heart.

Back at the cabin, we put the final pieces of the jigsaw together only to realize that the last piece was missing.

The next morning, I watched Mick sleeping on the sofa, off in dreamland and snoring. I would be sad to lose this feeling. It felt 'family'. It was everything I had wanted from a brother. Now I would go back to the big empty country house and he would go back to the city. I made him a coffee and placed it by his bed, took my herbal tea and went outside.

We packed and headed for the plane. Mick was sad to leave. He had been surprised he had felt so at home. So at home, yet we had done nothing except just life. He had found me easy company. The feeling was mutual.

The plane stopped in New York and we had four hours for our connection to the UK. We left the airport, catching a taxi as the radio played Somewhere Out There. We arrived at the Empire State Building and caught the elevator up high into the sky to see forever. At the top we walked around within a glass cage that looked out on the early evening sky of bright lights. Mick was alive with it all. I felt vertigo, as though I was falling up here high in the sky. I clung to the wall like a wildcat.

As we left the sun was setting over New York, and we drove through the twinkling lights of the city.

On the plane back to the UK, I dared to ask Mick if I could lean on his shoulder. We both fell asleep. I awoke to the serving of breakfast and found myself asleep on Mick's shoulder. We looked at each other, our faces daringly close. I closed my eyes again and stayed there a while before sitting up, my heart racing.

On the ground again, now in the UK, we made our way to my hotel, Mick's tape playing Celtic sounds of drums and pipes and me wrapped up in the memory of the car drives in America. I would sleep off some of my jet lag before catching the train home, although here was home, here and now, and I felt time was ticking away. I had a twin room and Mick was welcome to sleep too before driving home. I made tea, he made coffee and we climbed into the single beds like a pair of children.

Mick took Travel Bear and held him to his ear.

'Really…No…She did…'

After listening to what Travel Bear had to say, Mick told me Travel Bear had told him he wanted to stay with him.

'No,' I said.

Mick insisted he and Travel Bear were good buddies and Travel Bear had told him he wanted to stay with him. I took Travel Bear back from him across the tiny gap that divided our beds and tucked Travel Bear in with me.

'Goodnight, Travel Bear,' Mick said.

Travel Bear stood for the child within me. Mick was right, that child in me had wanted to stay with him. He acknowledged that child in me and rather than seeing it as a wall between us, he saw it as a bridge. This man would never have encouraged me to dissect and discard my bear.

We awoke a few hours later, arranged a breakfast, ate, and left for the station. At the station Mick insisted on walking with me to the train and I climbed on with my bags. Mick got on too, blocking the entrance with the body of a rugby player. I looked at him and fought the excruciatingly difficult feeling of 'lemons'. I felt jolted doing this, and Mick, biting his bottom lip, his big chunky cheeks sitting high up on his face, looked pretty much like things weren't so much different for him as for me.

'Can I hug you?' I asked tentatively.

'Yes,' came the answer.

Well getting the words out was one thing, now my body had to act upon them. Mick's arms went out. I took the cue and dived in like he was a jelly. I pushed my body and face up close to him and he held my head against his chest like I was very loved. I breathed in experience like it would have to last me all the way back and for ever. The train was ready to leave and we stood back looking at each other as briefly as the 'lemons' of a jolted consciousness can endure. I was ready to sing and cry and stood there sad and blissed with some huge inaudible knocking at the door of my consciousness saying 'by God I want to be with you'.

Mick got off, waved and started to walk away, the shyness cheeks sitting high on his flushed face.

Back at the big empty farm, the honeymoon was over. With nobody to copy, my Exposure Anxiety reigned. Every time I wanted to eat, I was compelled to avoid, divert or retaliate against the need, leaving me starving, and some days barely eating at all. The toilet was the same, as was getting a drink or putting on a jacket. I used to be able to get a drink for Ian and snatch one for myself, grab one as a copy of him or out of compliance when he saw it as 'good for me'. Left to my own devices, merely becoming aware I wanted one meant I was instantly cleaning the floor, dusting the fireplace or scrubbing the rubbish bin, anything but getting a drink. I convinced myself I didn't want things so that the Exposure Anxiety would get off my back and free up the action. I used characterizations, chattering to myself as someone else and communicating with the glass and the tap, singing my way through the actions. I used the delivery of the toilet paper, soap or towels to the bathroom in order to cash in casually on using the loo which I had been compelled to avoid to the point of near peeing myself. I would dialogue with my jacket to manage to wear it by blaming the jacket for making me wear it.

I wanted out, and I didn't want to want that. I wanted to be strong. This was too big for me. This was all too big for me. I was going to need some help and as Mick was my only close friend, I didn't want this to be all put on him. Nor as a depressed but fun-loving guy of twenty-six did he have the time and space for that in his life.

The number at Social Services passed me on to another number and then another. I explained that I was a person with a developmental disability and that my father had recently died, my husband had left, I was going through huge and shattering changes and I needed some help to hold on. I explained that I didn't want a shrink or a social worker, I wanted someone to help me form developmental programmes. I wanted an occupational therapist.

An occupational therapist called. Her name was Beth and she was coming out to see me.

Beth arrived, and I used my rocks to explain the situation. I explained how I had my whiteboards and my notices but that I needed to get a programme together. I needed company, we agreed on that. More than anything, I needed social involvement.

'I could get a cat,' I suggested.

'A cat would be a start,' Beth replied.

I had liked Beth, she seemed down to earth, without trimmings or bullshit, and empathic, as though she had somehow known me. On her way out the door, I told her I was an author and suggested she take a copy of my first book to help her understand where I'd been and some of the mechanics I was working through. She looked at the floor and then admitted she had already read them.

'Oh no,' I said, 'not a fan.'

'I'm afraid so,' Beth replied.

There was a dance class advertised in the local town and run by a woman not far from where I lived. Beth and I had agreed that all I had to do was show up. We discussed the animals and how I was or, more to the point, wasn't coping with the pony and the pigs and the sheep and what I might be able to do about that. We discussed me getting a cat, and came to the conclusion that that probably was something I could cope with and would be grounding. We discussed dyslexia and difficulty telling a bill from an advertisement and discussed what I might do to avoid accidentally tearing up the bills and throwing them away. We discussed attention and organizational problems and some exercises that might help get one half of my brain talking a bit better to the other half. We discussed Exposure Anxiety in the absence of anyone to copy and agoraphobia and the challenges in trying to stay 'out there', especially on days when I felt so compelled to close myself away. We discussed co-dependency and keeping oneself safe from merging with the needs and wants of others. We made lists, and finally I could attribute responsibility to the lists and actually get things done.

Prince, the Shetland pony, acquired just weeks before Ian left looked like a cardboard cutout out in the field from where I stood at the window as it rained. I had wanted a horse which would be free to 'Simply Be' without expectation. I imagined it as a happy horse that would run and play in the fields. But Prince just stood staring into space in a state that looked sadly like autistic withdrawal. The poor animal had some kind of infection which made it itch terribly, and it needed brushing and washing down several times a day with a fungicide or its body would twitch and shudder continually with the itch. I just kept forgetting and didn't know how to comfort the poor guy.

I went out and had a word with Prince and told him I'd have to get him a better home. Then I got in the car and went down to a little shop down the road and put an advertisement up that Prince was free to a good home.

Back home I went back out to Prince and washed him with the fungicide and he seemed happy as I brushed his poor raw back where the infection had made his hair fall out and his skin dry and flaky and small flies buzzed about. I nuzzled my face to his velvet face as I brushed him. If only I could put an advertisement up for me, free to good home.

Driving down the road on the way to get a cat to live with, I was thinking back on where I had been and where I had now got to. I had an overwhelming sadness well up in me. I felt unworthiness.

What had happened to the poetry book? Had it been intercepted by anyone? Had my father's ex-girlfriend read the poem about what happened all those years ago? Even now as an adult, I was in terror of the potential consequences. It was always clear one should never talk of such things. I had seen what happened to the animals in that household, been made to help dig their graves. Even if one could, it was clear these things were meant to remain invisible, as though they never happened. What did I know anyway? That would be the official line. I had been a crazy child, labeled emotionally disturbed. I couldn't even talk straight back then. That would be the defense. And it was true that I lived in a world of ghosts where it didn't matter how many animals got killed around me. That was life, it just happened. In your own world it was all external stuff and dream-like, just like a tape recording except it was my own life. He'd told everyone he was being poisoned and the old lady who brought him sandwiches at lunch time had been blamed. And I had never told. But when finally somehow I stopped being made to stir the gravy, then, in my childhood world, of course it must all have stopped. Nobody was being poisoned, not without the gravy being stirred. As a child, what you don't see anymore of course has stopped.

And now here I was loving Mick and afraid in case he loved me back. Afraid that he might touch me in the real world and within my world and I'd have to embrace all I was and had been.

It was now pouring down with rain and someone was screaming. There was the most haunted screaming coming from somewhere close by, filling the car with its sound, sweeping me up in it. It was coming from me.

I pulled over to the side of the road and stayed there for about an hour letting the floodgates go. It was almost as bad as The Big Black Nothingness, the emotional fits I'd had most of my early childhood. My God, did I have loads of this stuff inside me, all just waiting for the connections that never came? Was this what would happen once the information-processing problems were progressively shoved out of the way? Would all the baggage of my childhood now pour down upon me?

Finally, the screaming had stopped. I lay against the car window, an arm around myself. I started the car again, heading off to bring me home a cat.

I arrived at the cats' home and was shown about. Cats clung from the chicken wire of their shared enclosures. A few walked about the grounds freely, some curled up with one another, some watching me like tiny wild cats in the grass. Some were not so well physically, some not so well psychologically or emotionally. One was fourteen years old, a sad tiny bag of bones with kidney disease whose carers had simply brought it in in order to get a new cat and just left it there, after fourteen years of loyalty. There were little kittens with lunatic wildness and indiscriminate smoochers who showed the same attention to anything which stood still long enough.

A sleek little panther had followed me around like a dog in peaceful silence by my side, as I went from cage to cage waiting for some magic that would tell me who was meant to come home with me. They were all so needy. Some because they craved love, others because they had had it and lost it, and others because they were so defensive against love.

A kitten flung itself at me from the other side of the wire. Another fell all over itself purring at what appeared the very thought of my proximity and the promise of being stroked. A cat lay at my feet on its back waiting to be tickled. Another purred around my legs. The panther sat and watched them all. When I moved, he moved with me like my shadow.

I couldn't decide. I felt I should take home so many: the bag of bones, the wild kitten, the idiot falling all over itself in oblivion. I walked back to the office a little despondent. The panther walked at my side.

'I guess that's it then,' I said to the panther, 'you've decided I'm yours.'

I reached down and picked him up. He responded as though he had always known me, as though he had waited for me. I wondered about his name. He didn't have a cat face really, more like a cat-dog. He had some Burmese in him and a definite elegance and sureness, and a sort of resigned humour. Monty. His name felt to be Monty.

'He's decided I'm his,' I announced in the office. They were glad, very glad. He had been there at the cats' home for years.

He was a strong, self-owning and proud 'Simply Be' personality, this cat. He was a serious cat and quite a loner. He had a good voice and he talked to me in cat. I called him Monty. He called himself *wrowl*. He also called me *wrowl* or *prrrrrrr* depending on his mood. He watched me sleep and I watched him sleep and he reminded me of Mick who also was crazy for hair brushing. Monty cuddled me with his long black cat arms and held my hand with his paw curled around it as he looked at me with his serious face and made me cry all the time. I talked to him about things and he didn't mind. I thought he was a good person. He thought I was too.

'This is one lucky cat,' said the woman behind the counter as I piled up the new cat basket, the scratch post, the feeding bowl, the cat litter tray and all the etc., etc.

I smiled to myself.

In the house, Monty immediately took a shit on the carpet smack in the middle of the entrance hall just inside the door. Well, that was a good start. He had made his statement loud and clear. This was HIS house.

Having been briefed already about this upcoming event, I understood, and scooped it up and whisked it away now it had served its purpose. Laying claim to the house was passable. I just hoped he now didn't have to lay claim to me. I had no desire to wake up to the smell of cat shit on my bed.

Exposure Anxiety now sensitized to the presence of my new company meant it took a while before I would pick Monty up again. He would purr around my feet and try to sit with me. I let him take responsibility for his own actions, but it was hard to be responsible for taking action upon him which I could not attribute to his asking.

Gradually, I started to hold this furry breathing creature which had
taken me so unconditionally as a friend, as his best friend. He would take
my hand in his paws, curling his paws around them like little hands
around my hand, and pushing his head underneath my hand, as if to
instruct me clearly that he wanted to be patted. He wanted attention and
to be special. I would pat him and he would look at my face as though
wanting me to look at him. Sometimes I did. I was sure that he was
smiling and it made me cry. He made life look so easy – feelings and
touch and being in company – all so easy.

The movement class started up and Margo, the instructor, said to
drop by her house and she would show me the way to the class. I
arrived and we bundled into her car. It wouldn't start. I said I would drive
her in mine. She nattered all the way, burbling over herself in contagious
giggles as though her mind was a big ball of unravelling wool.

The movement class was twenty minutes away as we drove through
the narrow, dark lanes, hemmed in by tidy hedgerows. All the way there,
we laughed almost non-stop.

Margo was a muddle-head of sorts, with wide, smiling eyes and an
animated face with a somewhat shy smile in spite of burbling like a
waterfall. She had a fairly light sort of a spirit, aged somewhere between
five and fifteen within a forty-something body.

The class was challenging, encouraging us to explore self-expression
and let out the feeling that was inside us. At times I felt on the verge of
panic, gripped and finding it difficult to breathe. After the class, Margo
asked if I wanted to come to the pub with the rest of them. I declined and
the suggestion fizzled out. I drove her home. She asked me in and we
chattered until late.

Margo's house was that of an old hippie. Everything was wood and
natural with a wood stove and the smell of burning logs and incense. She
offered me tea.

'Do you have herbal tea?' I asked, expecting the reply to be the usual
astonishment.

'I've got lots. What would you like?' she said pointing upwards at
bunches of flowers hanging from the ceiling and going to the cupboard
and exposing a row of tins filled with home dried herbs. 'There's
elderflower, yarrow, nettle, chamomile and ...'

'Nettle,' I replied. 'No, no. Yarrow. No, yarrow and nettle. Is that OK?'

'Does this fella know what you feel for him?' she asked.

'I think so,' I said, 'I wrote it to him.'

'And ...' she prompted.

'And nothing,' I answered. 'We're friends.'

'Friends?' she queried.

'Friends,' I replied.

'Is he interested in you?'

'I don't know. I think so, but he wants to be just friends, and anyway, I want to be just friends,' I replied.

'No you don't,' she retorted flippantly.

'Yes I do,' I answered back defending myself.

'No you *don't*,' she replied matter-of-factly. 'But if you think he's not interested, then it's not worth pursuing.'

I sat sipping my tea.

'Does he call you?' she asked.

'No,' I replied. 'That's not what he's like. He doesn't even phone his friends, he just meets them down the pub.'

'What is this guy, an alcoholic?' she laughed like a mocking big sister. 'Bet you're the child of an alcoholic.'

'Anyway, what do you mean?'

'You're a rescuer. You're making excuses for this guy,' she continued, pouring herself another cup. 'This is no good. No matter how much you win him, you'll never have saved your mother.'

'What does any of this have to do with my mother?' I asked.

'Did you want to save her?' she asked.

'I was terrified of her,' I replied.

'Did she act like she needed saving?'

'I couldn't have saved her.'

'So if you could rescue her, you'd have been safe,' Margo went on.

'I didn't try to rescue her. I brought home animals instead. I rescued animals.'

'And did you feel safer then?'

'No, they got killed.'

'So now you've got to try even harder.'

'Oh this is all Freudian,' I replied. 'What's this got to do with Mick?'

'Its about co-dependency,' said Margo. 'You're addicted.'

'Mick's a good bloke. If you met him you'd know.'

'I'm sure he is,' Margo said and smiled warmly. 'Anyway, if I met him I'd be angry with him. He's messing you about. You don't know if you're coming or going, and you're chasing your own tail.'

'Maybe I'm just messed up,' I said. 'It'll sort.'

When I went to leave, Margo tried to hug me and I cringed.

'We really have to work on that,' she said, her eyes smiling, her Mary Poppins voice bordering on a giggle. 'I'm a really huggy person.'

'I've always been like this,' I replied, 'especially with women.'

'Well, I send one with you, there you go,' she said laughing and throwing me a make-believe handful of hug.

Margo and I didn't live far from each other and we progressively became friends. I would go to her house and drink nettle tea standing by her wood stove. She was one to dare and get me to confront myself. Though equally flawed herself, she was aware of the secrets we all have from ourselves, our excuses and our cop-outs.

Margo's classes involved expressing yourself individually without someone to copy or follow. They involved letting your feelings out through movement and, worse still, through movement in relation to each other. They involved not compliance but initiating when each individual felt ready. I made her a copy of the tape Mick had made for me. She played it at her classes and we moved like wild things, creatively to the music, being part of it.

Margo smiled at me when I entered the room, and I felt the rush of lemons that silently screamed as my stomach contracted tightly filled with the rocks of dread.

It was a small class with the other four women my own age or older, all of them with fairly grown children. It was strange to think that I was just starting to get here and that if I had had children at the same age my mother had me they would now be in their early teens.

Josie was one of the women at the class. She was ten years older than me and the mother of five, most of whom were grown up. She had a good feel about her. She owned herself. She didn't seem to be seeking to know me but was open to it. She didn't look for her impact upon others, she just took things as they happened. Self-owning entities were easy for me to handle.

Margo put on the atmospheric music and the room began to feel safe, not really part of the rest of the world at all. Though Margo was a muddle-head and a manic puppy, she had a talent for creating a warm and non-invasive atmosphere.

After gently awakening our bodies, she had us awaken to the room, to explore it through our bodies, to feel it richly through our senses in a non-overloading way, moving among each other. She had us find the music within ourselves and let our bodies feel it and move with its patterns, its changes of pace and intensity and to use it as the vehicle of expression for our own feelings coming through our bodies. Finally, she had us meet each other within it.

Margo had the class use touch improvisation to the music, and we were paired off to explore trust and balance using one another's bodies. I was paired off with Josie.

At first, when Josie made contact with me, it caused an instinctual aversion. Outside of the stored learned role playing of a play, I didn't spontaneously touch strangers, and perhaps especially women.

When I fought my own aversion, a squeal rose in my throat, and I felt compelled to slap myself to save me from slapping Josie. I handled it, but the aftermath of the internal payback was too much and I removed myself from the group, jumping a bit to get the crazy erratic energy to disperse itself and stop causing a state of inner earthquake. We were to swap roles, the initiator to become the receiver, the receiver to become the initiator. I tried to breathe with my chest feeling encased in a concrete jacket. We moved to the music and the rhythm and I initiated touch as part of movement in relation to Josie. Again, the noises, the stifled scream getting closer to the surface. It was like taming a wild horse. I was conquering mountains in Margo's class, and it made me feel bold and strong.

I decided to sell the house and to buy a van. Monty and I could travel. I had an estate agent come and value the house and put up a 'for sale' sign, and I bought the buy-and-sell newspaper to look for vans. I found one and drove a few villages away to look at it.

It was a big lug of a thing, a big Bedford with an overhang at the front. It felt like I was driving a truck. I'd grown up around car yards and cars, climbing in vans and exploring them. Jackie Paper had had me 'drive' the car from the age of three. My brother and I had had an old wreck in the back garden which I'd got going, jolting my way across the garden before hitting the aviary. At the age of eleven he gave me the keys to his truck and, driving it alone in the field of his farm, I had hit a tree. He gave me the keys to his minibike and, not having asked or understood about brakes, I had thrown myself straight over his barbed wire fence. If nothing else, he had encouraged me to have no fear of moving vehicles. And in spite of serious visual perceptual differences, I didn't.

The next day the people selling the van showed up at the farm, and I wrote them a cheque and grabbed the house keys and my money. While they were still there, I closed up the house and got in the van so I followed them out the drive as they had arrived.

The van was monstrous huge. I felt like a little piece of fluff. It wasn't easy to drive and I hogged the road. It was lots of 'shit', 'damn', 'no, second gear, not reverse', 'stuff it, driving in third gear will do just fine', 'right, no dancing around corners', 'no, don't you dare play with the radio right now', 'no, that's a rule, DONT PLAY WITH THAT DAMNED RADIO YOU MANIAC!', 'indicators would be nice', 'right, where's the horn in case I need it', 'no, not the squirty thing', 'shit, now the windscreen's a mess, where's the wipers', 'oh so that's where high beam lives', 'watch out for the parked cars', 'was that my wing mirror?'.

I drove to the petrol station and worked out the mechanics of all that and got petrol all over the place. By the time I went to pay for the petrol, I was such a proud thing. I was certainly one foot taller inside. I headed back home, then I changed my mind and went further. I went to the supermarket and could see right over the hedges. I even parked at the supermarket doing something resembling parking. When I got out of the big van, there were three women my size all goggling and I just smiled to myself telling myself: 'Yep. I drove that truck. Look at it. I got that here and I'm driving that up to Newcastle to meet with Mick.'

I called Mick. He answered.
'I'd like to meet you up in Newcastle and show you the van. Want to come and stay in it?' I'd asked.

'Oh, and there's one more thing. I want to sleep with you and I won't know how to know if you want that so I'll just say that if you show up with a sleeping bag, I'll know you're not interested and if there's no sleeping bag then …' I finished.

I was dead proud of driving myself up to Newcastle, and even prouder I knew what I wanted and had managed to ask for it. A hundred times something in me screamed to turn around. I sang loudly making up a song called 'Today Starts Now', about the feel of Mick…

> *Where does time find you, in the morning left behind you, see those footprints, see those footprints in the sand… With the clouds you drift by, happy blue, own piece of sky… Well that's the way, the way to play it, if life is a dream, no need to wake it, yesterday's gone, today starts now, today starts now.*

I drove into the Caravan Park where I'd agreed to meet Mick. He pulled up alongside the van and I opened the door. He had a bag with him and a smile.

'No sleeping bag,' I said observing.

'No sleeping bag,' confirmed Mick.

Well, whatever Margo thought, he was interested.

We lit a candle and played cards till late. I climbed into silk pyjamas, and Mick was in his shorts, his thick hairy rugby legs protruding. It seemed amazing to me that he had never had a girlfriend, that girls had only ever wanted him as a friend.

Sexuality was awakening and I wasn't sure what to do about it. These were not logical agreements as they had been with Ian, agreements to explore for development's sake. This was plain sexual desire.

It's hard to explain the difference between an agreement to explore touch as a kind of therapy and simply having desire. But one is about learning how to tolerate being scratched without having the itch, the other is recognizing the itch and quite naturally knowing that a scratch is going to solve it. I had been through many sexual revolutions, through tolerating sex as rent throughout my intermittently homeless teens, to exploring the physical alone with a stranger whom I wouldn't let speak to me in my twenties. Then I had been in love with Shaun, the Welshman, but unable to dare sexuality with him, each of us far too exposed and overwhelmed by emotion. Then I had had a consensual agreement to explore touch with Ian. What I now had was an overwhelming warmth of closeness to this man, but I was not so overwhelmed that I couldn't feel the drive to make this physical. In fact, in spite of the grip Exposure Anxiety had over so many things, making this feeling physical felt essential.

I told Mick I was getting into bed. He brushed his teeth in the sink and got into bed in his T-shirt and shorts and lay next to me still and almost frightened. I snuggled back into his body feeling his breathing, wrapped up in the smell of him, sweating against him and him against me. He nuzzled into my hair, his hand held me around my middle. His lips touched my neck gently as if by accident. I reached back ruffling his short cropped hair and feeling his face like a blind girl, my fingers exploring his mouth as I turned to face him. I indicated he should take off his T-shirt. I removed my pyjama top and put my body up against his. I felt the form of his body within his shorts pressed close to my body and we kissed like lovers wild and hungry our clothes peeling off into the van. I felt alive and wild and wanting, and it was more than Mick could take. Things were over with before they really started. I was in so many ways still a virgin, and so, I expect, was he. And it could not have been better. I had been left wanting more, and this fed my new-found fascination like a gust of wind catching a spark and creating a wildfire.

We woke up in the middle of the night and passion took us like a tidal wave. I felt ready to freefall into the warmth of belonging and to finally know what I had wanted so much to know – what was lust in the arms of love? What was it like to so desire the depths of physical connection, to want so much to join with another human being and for it to be more than just a dream in one's own world? But before we got past the petting of teenagers, Mick was overwhelmed yet again, and I lay there tightly held by his wet shaking body and still feeling like a virgin. The next morning, the same thing. I had discovered I was a sexual tornado, but at this rate I'd never see the sex I had wondered about. With a kiss and a coffee, Mick left for work, lighting an eagerly awaited cigarette as he left the van. I kissed him back, amazed and in awe of what had been this strange and magical night, and absolutely hooked on this man from whom I'd likely never get the experience I was so curious about.

Back on the farm Monty purred as if my evening had been an eternity and looked disappointedly at his cat bowl as if to say 'more'. I felt somewhere between a giggle and a shout and picked him up and danced around the house.

Viewers came to look at the house, and Monty hid under the bed. I accepted twenty thousand pounds less than I'd paid for it and got rid of the thing. I had sixty days to find somewhere else.

Around at Margo's we celebrated over herbal tea, sharing stories of what had happened with Mick, the sale of the house and where exactly I thought I was heading to now.

'No idea,' I told her. 'But I've got this idea for a consultancy.' I explained my philosophy that the people who seek help would return to their own homes, so whatever help they received should be something they would take with them.

It was also my philosophy that training what were already weighed down camels didn't make sense, so any help would involve first removing the straws from the camel's back and that meant helping people to understand the biochemistry issues as well as the environmental changes.

I suggested that if people enquired they'd be informed that they'd have to be committed to change and not just toying with it, because it would make demands on them. With the help of my rock collection, Margo and I worked out all the practical concerns. I'd have to have a separate business and private number and the address of the consultancy would not be advertised. People would enquire to a PO box, and only if they requested an appointment would they be sent the address and directions. I dreamed the consultancy would be a community of special people who could work with auties in a 'simply be' way.

'So you wanna be a consultant with me?' I asked. 'You're dyslexic. That makes you a cousin. I open up with you. You'd be great. I would teach you what you're looking at.'

Margo said she'd have a serious think about it, that it sounded interesting.

'Where you gonna start this consultancy then?' she asked. 'I'll go get us a map.'

Margo returned with a map and a pin.

'I want to be somewhere in the middle of the UK,' I said, taking the pin and closing my eyes before striking the map.

'That's nice there,' said Margo, observing where the pin had landed. 'Great Malvern, the Malvern Hills, that'll suit you. It's full of eccentrics.'

A package arrived in the post, sent by Mick. I tore it open, my heart racing. I was so blissed that he would send me something. It was a video, the video of the documentary we had made, no note, just the video. I put it on. I played it through once then played it through again stopping at certain phrases. But it wasn't just the things Ian was saying and doing which jumped out so starkly, it was the part where Mick featured, briefly caught by the camera. It was so clear in the video, so much clearer than it had been being actually caught up in it.

'Hel-lo,' said Mick on the other end of the phone.

'Hi,' I replied.

'Oh, hi. What can I do for you?' asked Mick a little taken aback.

'I just saw the video,' I answered.

'Did you see that part where Ian says he's like barbed wire to keep the world out?' Mick returned. 'That really disturbed me.'

'Ian saw the world like something on the other side of a castle wall,' I explained. 'He was really proud of being "barbed wire".'

'Did you see that part when he said he would replace you with a dog if you died?' asked Mick.

I didn't tell Mick that I had seen him in the video too. I had seen him being friends with me and how I'd known he was behind me when I looked around like that. He had had a look of adoration and openness, biting his lip as he watched me, unaware he himself was being filmed. I saw the change in him when he had moved in front of Ian and figured himself within camera shot, and I hit the pause button on the video because Ian's expression was so far from warm. He looked rather bitey actually – like the dog and the postman. If I had any doubts that Mick had had feelings for me, here I had none. Still, not since the Welshman had I known someone so claustrophobic about commitment.

I saw Ian say that no-one understands me like him. I heard him say we haven't spent a single day apart in two years, and then I saw my hand held and my hand held and my hand held – with a cold neediness that wasn't mine. I saw him talk about the dinners made with the best of intentions that made me such a buzz-junkie that he felt he then had to control me for my own good.

Ian had told me to be very very cautious about sharing my world with people because they had to go and live in 'the world' – as though it would hurt them to know what else there was. He taught me it was wrong to let people be close to me in a way that doesn't fit among 'the worlders' because this would hurt the people.

'Did I take from you?' I asked Mick.

'No, you didn't,' said Mick warmly.

'Did I hurt you to get close to you?' I asked.

'Nope,' said Mick. 'We're friends.'

'The world is not full of people like me. Is that hard?' I asked.

'Sometimes,' said Mick. 'I haven't been the same since I got back from the documentary. I didn't know it would affect me like that. It was great, there was no bullshit and no expectation. It just got so hard for me back here after being there.'

'I think that the change was already there in you,' I explained. 'I didn't make it happen, just maybe meeting me caused some of it to come to the surface, speed up or whatever. It's like the fork in the road – you can go back down where you know but you can't undo that you stood at that fork and saw something different. I don't think I did your head in.'

'It wasn't that you did my head in,' said Mick. 'I just couldn't get back into my structure. It changed how I looked at my life.'

'Maybe some of that made it hard to motivate yourself towards further involvement associated with a place that already gave you bad feelings,' I said, trying to clarify things. 'Sort of like looking for gemstones by fossicking through shit – not easy, especially if your sense of smell is on-line and you realise, hey, this ISN'T mud!'

'Finding myself with big feelings in the middle of all that didn't make it easier,' said Mick quietly.

'My flitty life is partly helium. I am sorry if it put you on the spot and messed up your structure by my whirlwind ways,' I continued. 'I know we both avoid involvement. I just had big feelings.'

'Same,' said Mick briefly.

'In all the confusion, there are still things you do know. You know you like your job and you know you deserve and want and need a proper lockable Mick room where his things are safe to spread out with some permanence and to be among real people you feel OK with. You know you need some structure and a place of belonging and if you haven't got it, and if it is not to be "found", you know how and where to "make" it,' I rambled. 'Thanks a lot for helping me with my own chaos. You offered to hear mine when you had a mountain of chaos yourself. I never really helped much with yours. I did listen but I never really let you know that I did understand.'

'It's my problem,' said Mick, clarifying the boundaries.

'You want to come up here for a visit some time? I sold the house. I've been talking to Margo. I'm gonna start a consultancy. I thought about going to live up north,' I burbled.

'Don't move up here on account of me,' interrupted Mick quickly. 'I don't know where I'm going. I'm off to Thailand next year.'

'It wasn't because of you,' I replied. 'I also thought about going to Worcestershire. There's a place there in the hills Margo thinks is really nice. It's full of hippies.'

'Sounds nice,' said Mick.

'Want to come and say goodbye to the house and meet Monty?' I asked.

'I'd love to, but I don't know what I've got happening,' said Mick. 'Maybe next weekend or something.'

'Mick, I need to ask you something,' I announced quietly.

'No problem,' said Mick.

'I need to know where I stand,' I said. 'Are you in or out?'

'Look, you need a commitment, I can't give you that,' said Mick as my heart sank like a stone. 'I guess I'm out.'

'I understand,' I said, feeling stunned.

'Still friends?' asked Mick.

'Yeah sure,' I replied. 'That's what we always were.'

'Seeya,' I said ending the call.

'Yeah, you too, mate,' said Mick.

Two weeks had passed by as the rain set in and Margo and I sat in front of an open fire sharing sisterhood.

'So when you seeing Mick?' asked Margo patting Monty.

'Was meant to be last weekend,' I said. 'He's busy.'

'Busy in the pub,' said Margo.

'I don't know,' I replied, knowing she was most likely right.

'It's like a drug, you're addicted,' said Margo gently. 'You have to wean yourself off. Just don't call him for a while. Call me.'

'You're not him,' I laughed.

'I know,' she said. 'Being in love is like a sickness when it's not returned.'

'I thought it was,' I said.

'Maybe it was,' said Margo. 'But this guy's never gonna tell you what you want to hear.'

'What's that?' I asked.

'That he loves you. Did you do as I said? Did you ask him whether he's in or he's out?' she said gently.

'He said he's out,' I replied.

Then we talked about her dance class and my ideas for a consultancy. We talked about a new textbook I was writing about information processing problems. We talked about my upcoming trip to the hills of Worcestershire and about writing a musical together and how I would do the music and she would do the choreography. I played the guitar a little and sang her a song called 'Simply Be'.

> I feel part of the moon and the sun, of the colours surrounding me,
> And I am moved by the way nature plays its own music, the sparkles upon the
> sea.
> When you smile with your eyes I believe you're caught, caught in its symphony.
> And I can find no place I'd rather be.
> Some things will never change.
> Freedom is my middle name.
> If this is crazy, don't give me sane,
> Let me Simply Be.

'You have a beautiful voice,' she said.

I shrugged.

'Seriously, how many of these songs have you got?' she asked.

'Heaps,' I replied. 'Probably about fifty.'

'When you get settled, you should make a CD,' she said. 'Seriously.'

I played another song, a song called 'Sometimes' which I had co-written with Julian all those years ago. Margo sat and closed her eyes as she stroked Monty now on her lap.

> Sometimes, you ask is it worth it,
> To want to be with one who wants to be free.
> And then, sometimes, she says 'yeah, it's worth it'
> If only for something it brings out in me.
> And then I hide in the words that I've poured onto paper,
> Sing to the faces who don't know I'm there,
> And then I hide in the music where there's no danger,
> And I sing to the faces who don't really care.

'That's amazing,' said Margo. 'You don't need this fella. You've got so much more ahead of you. Do you think you'll ever have children?'

'I like them, but can you imagine it?' I replied. 'They'd be chasing me about for things. I'd be hiding, trying to get away. They could have the same difficulties as my mother or my father or the Exposure Anxiety I've struggled with all my life. Mick wanted kids one day.'

'Irish, isn't he?' she asked.

'Yep,' I replied.

She said nothing a while, then: 'You gonna be OK if you never hear from him again?'

'He says we're friends,' I replied, 'I can call him.'

'Don't chase this guy,' she warned me. 'It's not good for you.'

I drove up to Great Malvern to look at a house that was both up for rent and for sale, out on the outskirts of a village. It was off down the beaten track, a stream running along the back garden, surrounded by forest with only one street of houses in the middle of nowhere. It was a tiny wooden miner's cottage surrounded by nettles with one bedroom, rattling windows and mice in the walls. It was ideal. Monty and I would be OK here, and I would run the consultancy from the shed under the house, which was currently full of spider webs and rubble and 'just needed a little love'.

Margo was happy and sad. We had become the best of friends and she saw me as a sister.

'Look,' I said, 'I'll get this consultancy up and running and you'll come up and do some training and, besides, there's also this talk coming up in Orlando. Mick hasn't got back to me yet. If he's not going, you want to come along? We can visit Disneyworld. Jean's gonna be there. She's nice.'

'I'd love to,' said Margo. 'You let me know.'

I would miss Margo's house, her little Jack Russell terrier that put its paws over its eyes when it slept and was kind to Monty when she came to visit us. I would miss being treated like a sister and the easy upfront way Margo had about her. I would miss the warmth of her smile and her solid boundaries.

I piled Monty into the van in his basket. The removal firm would deliver the rest of my things in a small van around the same time as Monty and I got to the new house. On the way I sang as Monty meowed:

*It's five a.m. and the clock just went three,*
*I'm turning quite ballistic and the cat's got fleas again.*
*I'm feeling kind of wild, feeling like I'm going insane,*
*And I just hung all the clothes outside and now it starts to rain …*
*I'm packing up, shipping out,*
*Lost my mind without a doubt.*
*Get off my case, get out my face,*
*I'm moving on.*
*This atmosphere has got me moving out,*
*I'm moving on.*
*Leave my mind alone,*
*I'm moving on.*
*Don't keep me on the phone,*
*I'm moving on.*
*Moving on.*

Not long into the new house Monty sat watching the mice amble across the threadbare carpet of the lounge room floor and the wind make the wooden house creak and almost sway. A knock came at the door and an old man and his pixie wife stood on the doorstep in the cold. They had come to introduce themselves, Fred and Jean, a rather ancient Brummy couple from up the road. The old woman's eyes met with mine and we recognised a kind of something in each other. They invited me to pop in for a cup of tea.

Fred and Jean were everything I needed. It was as though my grandparents were back from the dead and living just a few doors down. I patted their equally ancient dog as Jean told me how she didn't like a lot of people but 'you're alright, I like you'. She had a kind of something in her eyes, a glint, a sparkle. Jackie Paper had had it. His mother had had it. Sometimes I had it. We'd recognised it in each other.

'You see ghosts,' said Jean. 'I can see it in you.'

Fred stifled a giggle suggesting he go make a fresh cup of tea. He smelled the nettle tea I had brought.

'You sure this isn't just grass,' he laughed. 'Methinks you've been ripped off. How much they make you pay for this down the health food store? I got plenty of this out the back yard. I'll just go fetch me lawnmower.'

'I've seen ghosts,' Jean went on, 'and I see into people. You know what I mean. I can see you do it too.' She waggled a finger towards me.

'So what brings Donna to our village?' said Fred bringing back the tea.

That evening, I shut down the computer, closing the lid of my laptop on my newest book and sat watching TV in the house, the wooden boards creaking with the wind outside. There was an Elvis special on the TV, and I felt deeply in the company of my father as I watched it, a man who had loved to do Elvis impersonations. 'Come on, Polly, let's rock and roll', I remembered him saying almost as though he had just said it again, and I remembered how he would grab me by the hand and make me dance whether I liked it or not. I found myself crying and got up and danced like I was dancing then. The dead are never gone, they just become stronger in our own inner world and less present in the external world.

That evening my father appeared in my dreams. He was naked and filled with shame at his selfhood. He took me down a cobblestone lane to where there were two windows across from each other. He was afraid and shaking, and in silence I told him not to fear. I had him look into one window. It was full of images of him as a womanizing wheeler-dealer. Then I had him look across at the other telling him, like Scrooge, this is who he could have been. I told him to feel no shame and to walk proud. He talked about his cancer. I woke up both warmed and afraid and lay there a while telling him within myself that I was sorry.

I undertook my own therapy, seeing a woman who did McTimony chiropractic. It was a technique which involved manipulating the body to find where there were energy blocks and for getting the different parts of the body back in dialogue with each other.

It had been a few years before when a therapist at the Brain Injury Rehabilitation and Development Unit had done some testing and found that I still had infantile reflexes which were meant to have become inhibited back in infancy to make way for the development of later reflexes associated with other learning and development. I was still experiencing agoraphobic responses when people saw me outdoors, and I wondered if McTimony, which was used to help animals, would be able to help me.

The therapist had me lie down on the table. She raised and lowered different limbs, fist individually, then in relation to each other. Her actions caused reflexes to fire in response, and it seemed as though she would balance these limbs at certain points until a shot of electricity seemed to fire between the two. The process brought out a range of very spastic emotions, with growling and squealing rising in my throat and my arms and legs flailing occasionally in response to the uncomfortable reconnections. I felt embarrassed and apologized. She said it was no problem, that animals had similar responses and that it was natural. I was curious and asked her about the process. She explained that people think that traumatic experiences are stored in the brain but that in fact they are stored in the body. She explained that although it sounded irrational, I may have stored the memory of a particular trauma in my shoulder or my knee or a joint. Then we get defensive about freeing up the re-release of this trauma, so we end up with the different parts of our body disconnected. What her method was doing was reintroducing the different parts of the body to each other, and with that came a release of emotions associated with the original trauma they had reacted to. She felt that if someone stored enough of these it could impair their relationship to their body and clog up their capacity to properly process incoming information. After six weeks of this therapy, I found myself taking my dinner outside and waving to people as they went past. Whatever it was, something, however small and for whatever reason, had shifted.

I finished my book and called it *Connections*, outlining what I saw as the three faces of autism: problems of tolerance, problems of connection and problems of control. I wrote of Exposure Anxiety and an indirectly confrontational approach in turning around these involuntary avoidance, diversion and retaliation responses. I wrote of reducing sensory overload and speeding up information processing via dietary intervention as a key to reducing the degree to which these children were monotracked and their sensory fragmentation in response to information overload. I wrote about problems of impulse control and ways of channelling seemingly unwanted behaviours into productive activities.

As with *Nobody Nowhere* I made no overt reference to autism in the title but found myself faced with the insistence to change it. I saw it as a book for all people not exclusively those labelled autistic. But though the publisher loved it, she felt it had to be renamed. I was simply too famous in the ever-growing field of autism. So, 'Connections' slipped off its cover and overnight it re-emerged as *Autism: An Inside-Out Approach*. Just as I had rocked the literary world with *Nobody Nowhere* as one of the first published works by an able person diagnosed with autism, now I would rock the world with a self-help manual which detailed strategies for sensory-perceptual problems, being mono, delayed information processing and sensory and emotional hypersensitivity. The book was accepted instantly by my new publisher, Jessica Kingsley, and would go on to become a bestseller, reshaping the way people worked with and understood not just the experience of autism, but its underlying mechanics.

The book took off like lightning, and all I had to do was tell people how they could contact me. Where people had kept me writing four hours a day in answer to their questions, they had now inspired me to put all those answers into a book so people worldwide could have those answers too. I made up flyers about the new consultancy and sent them out to the big organizations. I let people know I was available to talk about my textbook, to run workshops on the concepts and strategies within that book, and I let them know I was available to see some of the families who had been writing to me in the hope that the experiences of my earlier development might hold keys to how they worked with their own children. Then I set about clearing spider webs and rubble down in the basement, hammering up partition board and laying some carpet tiles on the floor. I dragged a desk down and ran a spare phone line under the house and had my very own office.

Before long the phone rang and I was out in my van giving lectures in which I introduced people for the first time to my model of the 'three faces of autism': the system of sensing versus that of interpretation, being mono and delayed information processing, and the concept of involuntary fight-flight responses which I called Exposure Anxiety. The more I spoke, the more I found myself travelling across the country to visit families in their homes: a five-year-old who was meaning-deaf and high as a kite because of food intolerance; a three-year-old with severely fragmented visual perception overwhelmed by movement, change and visual chaos; a twelve-year-old phobic of social contact with desperate emotionally clinging parents whose identity and status hung on their child's every response. I observed families, sensory environments, the mode of communication and how directly confrontational interaction was. I observed these children's defence mechanisms, the language of their behaviour and how it interplayed with that of their parents. I wrote reports outlining altered approaches and informed parents about the role of diet and supplements in the treatment of autism. I began to hear back that some of the children showed drastic improvements, becoming more communicative, less defensively reactive, less sensorily avoidant, better able to keep up. Some of my self-injurious kids had become less self-abusive, a boy had begun to recognize his sister as a person for the first time, children with visual fragmentation began to relate to objects as a whole, a boy with no interaction began to help with the cooking and hang out the laundry out of his own curious volition and a child here and there began to speak. I was earning a reputation that spread like wildfire and the phone rang day and night. My approach was working where conventional approaches had failed. People wanted to hear more.

Monty walked about the nettles, paw-deep in snow as Margo arrived for Christmas. She had brought along her cat-loving terrier and we set about cooking roast dinner before cutting ourselves a branch off a tall conifer and taking it inside as our Christmas tree. I had some string and some plastic cows, so we tied them up around the middle and hung them on the tree. Then we twisted tin foil and folded paper to make little hanging spirals and fans before finally grabbing rice flour and throwing it all over the tree, ourselves and Margo's little dog pretending it was snow.

Margo had brought Monty a present, and I had bought one for her little dog. We gave them their presents and went out walking.

The Orlando trip was approaching and Mick had been out of my life now for quite a while.

'You want to come to Disneyworld with me?' I asked Margo. 'We'll meet with Jean too. She's fab. You'll like her.'

Margo sparkled and became an excited puppy.

'Of course,' she said full of beans. 'When is it?'
'Mid-February,' I replied.

I had signed up at the local arts college where they ran a sculpture class. It was run by the original grey-haired, mad artist called Clifford, and no sooner did I have my hands on a wodge of clay than I churned out a sculpture of Mick, nude in all his glory, head tilted dreamily off to the side with a Mona Lisa hint of a smile. Then I created my second piece, a little house up high on a rugged hill full of caves. Finally, I moved on to my third piece, a life-sized nude called 'My World–The World' in which I appeared lost in my own world, pushing out the external world and unaware I was exposed and soul-naked before the world looking on. My hands moved over her body, feeling each curve intimately until each limb, each facial feature, each stream of hair 'felt right'. I bandaged up each piece in turn, keeping the clay moist as this powerful woman seemed to produce herself through my hands.

In the street I began to notice faces and breasts and bodies and legs. I wanted to touch these women as living sculptures just as I had as a child in the cemetery, feeling the statues of angels and sitting with them, curved into their stony bodies.

My life-sized woman was my goodbye to that state of oblivion which would never be mine again, and it soon became the talk of the college. I felt like I had finally brought my mirror image to life, made her three-dimensional so I could stroke her face, my face, outside of myself, hold her in my arms as I so wished to be held by someone as familiar as myself. Every dimension of her was taken from the form of my own body, the face a replica of my own face in that pose. She took me six weeks and by the end a film crew arrived from the local news programme to witness this amazing sculpture, done in a few weeks by someone who had just started sculpture. In an instant, I had become notorious once again.

It was time to head off to the USA. I left Monty in the capable care of Fred and Jean, Margo left her terrier Poppy with her friend in Wales, and the two of us met up at the airport for our flight to Orlando. We talked about the consultancy and made excited plans to write a musical together. We talked about Mick and, more to the point, about his absence, and we talked about being a pair of muddle-heads on a trip to the USA.

The flight to Orlando was great fun, with Margo excited like a mad puppy pointing at things out of the window, her face beaming with a smile so big she looked in danger of swallowing her own head at times. We arrived in Orlando and made our way to the hotel, meeting with Jean, who seemed instantly at ease with Margo as did just about anybody. We cooked together like three sisters and went out seeing the sights, Ripley's Believe It or Not!, a nature park with rabid squirrels who chased us teeth gnashing, a donut shop where Margo and Jean dunked donuts in coffee and I watched politely, and a skating rink where we all skated on ice together in this sub-tropical American state.

The next day we headed for our day at Disneyworld before the big conference. It rained on us like the sky was telling us to go back home and the wind bit into us like an invisible ghost with teeth, and we laughed and laughed. We hadn't figured on my dietary wheelchair and there wasn't any food I could find that was clearly part of my diet. As hypoglycemia began to set in, I became dazed and disoriented, my fingers and lips numb and blue. I grabbed some fries, seasoned with who knows what and scoffed them down, telling Margo and Jean I'd be fine. Whether an allergic reaction or epilepsy brought on by the low blood sugar, twenty minutes later they were in the company of someone who looked like she had taken drugs. They blended with the multitude of strangers around me, their words meaning nothing. We were on a horror ride when the impact really took a hold, and I came out the other end thinking vaguely that we had seen monsters in there as though it was someone's house we just visited in real life. Margo and Jean discussed what to do. They could keep hold of me to make sure I didn't stray off in this drug-like state as I buzzed and squealed at the patterns and coloured lights around me. They could try to get me some water and clean food to try to diminish the effects. We headed off to get me straightened out.

After a load of water and plain unseasoned vegetables I had a thick head and was somewhat hungover, but back in the land of the living. We headed back to the apartment, made an open fire on this blustery day, and Jean and Margo roasted marshmallows as I looked on happily from the view afforded me by my dietary wheelchair.

Another day, Margo and I had a fight over some acorns. I was utterly willful and she was utterly disgusted with my willfulness, until finally after the layers of frost were thickening to iceberg level, she made me see that our friendship was worth more than this and I came down from my high horse into the arms of humility.

**B**ack home, I was glad I had travelled with Margo and wished that Mick had been as stable and silly as she was. I craved female company, a buddy old chum with whom all the in-love stuff wasn't an issue. I began to realize I wanted, so wanted to feel physically safe with a woman, to let go and fly like I had wanted to fly with Mick but with none of the complications, no broken heart. But Donna Williams couldn't be gay. The autism world would fall on its face with shock if their fairytale princess was interested in women.

One thing for sure was I was not in love with women. I fell for men, plain and simple. But sexuality was different. On the one hand it was everything to do with being in love. On the other hand, it was everything to do with companionship, loyalty and having fun, and I associated that with equal potential to both men and women.

The sexuality I had felt towards Mick now brought me only heartache. I had been unwanted, left aside, for whatever reason had made mental or emotional sense to Mick. Now I began to notice women's bodies, their flow and form, the different way they sat in their bodies to men. I noticed that some women didn't sit in their bodies like most women. It was as though they sat in their bodies as 'people', as though their gender didn't figure. I became fascinated by these androgynous folk. One such lived in the town, and I had been in the shop she worked in and got swept up in the feel of her. At home I fought with these feelings, certain I'd never make them public, that these were a private world thing and there was no reason to live such feelings. But my body wasn't listening. As far as it was concerned, it was awake and ready for the world and a man had broken my heart.

I contacted Gayline. I needed to understand this. The man on the other end of the phone kept referring to his lesbian friends and each time I pulled back from the word. I was fine about other people being lesbians but I was not 'one of them'. He gave me the number of a women's group in my area where I might meet women who would understand what I was experiencing. I wrote down the number.

I hid the number as though the number itself shouted out that dreaded word 'lesbian'. I hid the number as though Monty might see it and look strangely at me. I hid the number as though the world were watching over my shoulder with a look of disapproval. But in me I knew that I had a need to know what it was to be close to a woman, to enjoy the smell of one close to me, to want to be held by one.

Monty came and purred around my feet. It didn't matter a damn to him. I picked him up and tried out the word, announcing 'lesbian' to see if he flinched. Then I called him a lesbian. Then I told him I was a lesbian. Then we agreed we didn't like the word lesbian but we were OK with the word gay. I had had two very close gay male friends, so being part of their club sat fine. I decided that I was most likely feeling like I was a gay man in a woman's body.

By day, the phone rang and I booked talks and workshops and took details for trips out to visit families. By night, I felt sad that I couldn't even tell Margo, believing that these people who listened to me so eagerly would turn their backs on me if they knew that my new-found sexuality was progressively fixated on being with a woman.

Finally, I phoned the number I'd been given by Gayline. A woman answered and invited me over. She was part of a long-term, stable lesbian couple who shared the children she had from a previous marriage. They were nice people: warm, friendly and had herbal tea. I felt at ease with them, and when asked I could not lie about what I did for a living. One of the women was a social worker who worked with children with autism.

'You're not Donna Williams, are you?' she asked.

My nightmare was realized.

'Yes, I'm afraid so,' I replied.

Then she told me how much my books had helped her in her work. We discussed how her colleagues didn't know about her sexuality either and whether or not I thought that gender identity problems could cause autistic withdrawal. I said I didn't know.

Until my late twenties I had always lived as the 'my world' characters of Willie and Carol. As Willie, I felt male; as Carol, I felt female; as myself, I felt neutral. Willie was the embodiment of logic, my left-brain thinking unable to integrate with my right-brain thinking that I associated with Donna and self. Carol was my imitation of girls and a social façade of 'normality'. As Carol I had tolerated an early life of domestic prostitution, forced to live with men as an alternative to the streets. But my sexuality with Mick was mine, it felt like it came from me. Was it possible that my progressively more integrated left-brain self had its own version?

I went home with a feeling of achievement. My god, I had met lesbians, met them and they knew my name and they knew who I was and their heads didn't fall off or anything. But a question kept raising its ugly head. How was I going to meet someone? As in 'How was I going to *meet* someone?'

Though I didn't want my recent realization to become more real, I couldn't help the feelings that did. Fred and Jean, my new grandparents just a few doors down, were traditional old folk, they would never understand. Margo would maybe understand, and in fact had herself had affairs with women, but what if she thought she had somehow caused all this, even imagined that I was interested in her?

I threw myself madly into my work, beginning what would be my second textbook under the working title *The System of Sensing: The Unlost Instinct*. It was a book, inevitably to be repackaged as *Autism and Sensing*, and was about the world before interpretation, mind and concepts, in which we rely on the more right-brain reality of pattern, theme and feel. Finally, I dedicated the book to my father and grandmother, who probably never lost their minds because they were probably never fully committed to having them in the first place.

But no matter how busy I kept myself, how ferociously I merged with the process of writing or how run off my feet I was with the consultancy, my own personal issues wouldn't go away. I was still human after all.

After a number of weeks I phoned the couple I had met.

'Do you know where I could meet someone?' I asked.

They gave me the details of a club that got together once a month. Oh my god, no, I thought, go to a club and pick someone up. The thought gripped my gut. It was horrendous. I couldn't possibly. Not me.

It was the night of the club and I had driven my van part-way there three times and turned back, each time crying, knowing that I would eventually have to face it and that ignoring this was not a choice. Finally, I decided to go inside, order some sparkling water, drink it and leave.

I entered, paying my money at the door, and made my way to the kitchen. It was a small place with low lighting, and the music was not too loud. Only in the kitchen were there fluorescent lights and my tinted lenses took care of those.

There was a woman there, younger than me, in her twenties. She was a big person, like a female version of Mick, spiked hair, Doc Martens, the stereotype young lesbian. She was shy and defensive and she smiled briefly, looked away and left the room. In an instant I had mapped her, felt her walls and her fragility, her hope and her tragedy. Her Exposure Anxiety was worse than mine, and I felt empowered by that. This almost male sexuality I was feeling was foreign, but I trusted it as my body moved into the music hall with my drink. The woman held her drink tightly. All of her body language said she was gripped with dread of being approached, and yet something else seemed to be saying 'pick me'. I went over to her and sat down and introduced myself. Her name was Shelly. She looked at me briefly and guzzled down her drink like an alcoholic. Having grown up in an alcoholic home, they were familiar to me. I was a magnet for them.

I danced with the music, merging with it as she danced in the world like a moth getting closer to a flame. In the darkness of the room, I felt caught up in the music and the lights and her shyness empowered me. Shelly had drunk quite a bit and I felt for her. I asked her if she would like a lift home. She said that she would, but changed her mind on the way, asking me to pull into a parking area off the road. We sat in the back sitting opposite each other as she looked at her hands confiding that she had hoped I wanted her to come over to my place. I felt for her for some reason and felt what she wanted from me. I leaned forward and kissed her and she kissed me back. I asked whether she wouldn't rather go home having drunk so much. She confided that she lived with her lesbian mother who was an alcoholic and there would only be fighting there if she went home. I took her, like a stray kitten, to my place.

Shelly made herself at home, kicking off her Doc Martens and lying on my bed. I knew how to lie next to a female, I was used to that from staying with female cousins, from my feral days climbing into Terry's bed to escape the violence at home and from my teens living around the streets when I had a few inches in Robyn's bed for as long as my Exposure Anxiety would allow me to stay. But neither of them had had such a feeling about them, so alone, so desperate to be close and to belong. I felt such empathy within the similarities shared with this stranger.

The fact that Shelly was shy and rather drunk made my own Exposure so much less. I didn't explain that I had never been with a woman before. I didn't have to. I simply went to bed and left Shelly to make her own choices. She climbed in next to me and snuggled up behind me.

Shelly was soft and snuggly, her touch was slow and sensual. However else she would be a taker, in bed she was a giver, and we both were. I didn't care who she was. All that mattered was that she felt OK being here and was in charge of her own sexuality. It was the closest I would know to sleeping with myself as a separate body for in whatever ways we were so very different in how we had addressed the challenges life had thrown our way, sexually we were like mirror images of each other. We enjoyed each other like two kids gorging themselves on chocolate all night. Shelly confided that she had found what she had been seeking all her adult life, an orgasm. I may never have had this with a man, but here I too had discovered it with a woman.

The next day I treated Shelly like any stranger who happened to be in my house. I offered her breakfast. I had no bread, no milk, no sugar, no coffee, and after one look at my cupboard she declined, accepting a glass of water. She asked me about my work, about my background, about men. She told me about herself, chronic unemployment, a background of pleasing the men who wandered into her house, hitting upon a child home alone. She told me about picking people up in pubs just to have someone to talk to, about playing women's basketball, being a snooker champ, and about when she 'became' a lesbian. She was pretty as she spoke, expressive in spite of the damper of depression. She was self-effacing and compelled me to want to prop up her fragile sense of self, to shine light into the hopelessness of the world she portrayed. I felt a deep empathy for her. I didn't love her, nor was I in love with her, yet I didn't have to be. The empathy I felt for her consumed me. If I could have taken a chunk of my life and given her some of it, I would have.

I called Margo, and she told me how her classes were going. We talked about the consultancy and I began to cry. She said it didn't matter that I wanted to close it down, what mattered was that I was holding myself together. I didn't know where to begin, but I needed to know that someone in the world knew what I was going through and thought it was OK. I told her I had realized I was interested in women, as in physically. She said very little. I told her about meeting Shelly. She said that was great and that she hoped it worked out better than it did with Mick. I asked if she was still my friend.

'You haven't changed,' said Margo. 'You're just learning more about yourself. Anyway, how you finding it, the sex that is?'

I nearly fell on my face. Was the hang-up all in my head? Were people really as human and accepting as Margo? Had I worked myself up into a state for nothing?

It had been a few days since I had driven Shelly home when a letter arrived in the post, small rough writing with the odd crossing out. I opened it and read a tentative and hopeful letter, reaching out yet self-protective. It was a love letter. I had a love letter from a woman.

I didn't know how to respond. The feeling was not mutual. I liked Shelly and my empathy for her engulfed me, but I had never envisioned being in a relationship with a woman, an ongoing relationship.

Finally, I called, with each of us stilted, self-protective. She was shy, I felt responsible and the stray kitten complex took hold of me. She wondered if I would like to come over. I said yes.

Ashtrays overflowed surrounded by coffee cups. A deep fat chip fryer sat in a corner caked with grease. The house smelled of beer. I was introduced to her mother and was struck by the similarities this woman had with the feel of my own mother. I wanted to grab Shelly and run out of there whether I loved the girl or not.

I couldn't stay, nor could I just leave her there. In spite of her big-boned frame she looked so fragile, so hopeful I would want to know about her life, so afraid, almost pre-emptive, that I would not.

It was only days later that Shelly stopped going home. I felt kind of relieved but also trapped. I hadn't meant to be in a relationship and I didn't have what Shelly so needed me to give: the ability to say 'I love you' to her.

She began to put me down about my hair, about my teeth, about my breath, about the way I spoke, about my clothes, about how pale I was, how rundown my house was, how alone I was. The insults were subtle and constant, as though she was uncomfortable and struggling and could only feel equal by making these comments. I would explain that these were abusive and she would apologize, justifying herself as simply stating the facts. I pointed out that there were facts I could point out about her but didn't. It didn't seem to help. No sooner had she been so very sorry than she compulsively started all over again. Yet it was familiar too. She was voicing all the self-hatred I could ever muster and projecting it onto me. I may as well have been listening to the worst of myself. I was seeing elements of my mother.

I was still busy travelling all over the country and had attended a final conference in Scotland. The crowd took a break and were conversing with each other, busy friendly people keeping up with multitrack conversations about life. The isolation I was feeling was like a straitjacket tightening on me. I didn't need Shelly, I needed Margo. I could have coped with this isolation with her cheeriness bouncing along as a co-consultant.

I got a call on my mobile phone, it was Margo's adult daughter. Margo was in hospital. She had been hit over the head that night and had made it over to her neighbour's house before collapsing. She had had a brain haemorrhage.

'Is she going to be OK?' I asked, feeling helpless.

'She's back with us for now,' said the daughter, 'but she's in and out. She might not recognize you. She sounds a bit confused.'

I explained I was up in Scotland and that I couldn't get back straight away, but I got the number of the hospital and called and spoke to Margo.

She was her same old self and she talked about Orlando and about the musical we said we were going to write together. She talked about having come home in the dark, that she must have knocked her head. She talked about her daughter's being there and seeing her friends. She said she missed me.

The next day, Margo was dead.

I felt stunned and isolated by this year of death and upheaval. My closest friend, my only close friend, was gone from her body. I remembered the boyfriend she had been obsessed by, the one who had been jailed, and wondered if he would come after her. It didn't matter now.

She was gone from the physical world. The friend who had saved my soul was gone from that rustic hippie house and the life I had known her in. She would now live on only within my own world and the inner worlds of all those whose lives she had touched, immortal and ever there. I went and sat up on the hills in the wind to say goodbye to the lived life she had had. The wind itself reminded me of Margo, wild, adventurous, so very there and now invisible. I felt within her company within myself. I told her I would do the musical for her one day. Then I wrote a song:

> *Sleeping Beauty slept, she never heard the castle fall,*
> *And all the things she could have been, were just graffiti on the wall.*
> *Destiny had knocked but no-one answered to the call.*
> *Time is a thief which steals the chance that we never get to take.*
> *It steals them while we are asleep.*
> *Let's make the most of it while we are still awake.*

That night Margo appeared in my dreams telling me to tell her daughters that she loved them.

Shelly flicked through the TV magazine in the other room. I felt like she was all I had now.

'What you doing?' asked Shelly as I heated up an old wax candle in a pot within a second pot of water.

'I'm gonna try and make a candle,' I told her.

Shelly began to cut string for wicks and set up some cookie moulds for the small floating candles I was going to pour out.

I left the room for the loo, having held on for hours till I was about to pee myself, so Exposure Anxiety had finally let me go. When I returned, Shelly had made all the candles.

When they were set, I congratulated her. She was proud of them, suggesting we take them over to show her mother, that she could try to sell them.

This was the first time I'd seen her enthusiastic or proud of anything she had done, so I found a shoebox for them and we packed them in paper and took them over to her mother's place.

Her mother was busy with her own stuff, and her brother, hungover from the night before, looked through the candles, impressed with his sister's handiwork. He suggested they were good enough to sell, that she could make some money making candles. Shelly despaired that this was all she would have as she didn't have the money to buy a candle-making kit.

Shelly stayed back at home for the night and I determined to find her a candle-making kit. I found one at the art shop and took it back home.

Shelly had had enough of being back home and was ready to return. When I gave her the candle-making kit she was like a child at Christmas. By the end of the afternoon she had used the whole kit up and had a second shoebox full of candles.

'Do you really think they're any good?' she asked.

'Yeah, I do,' I replied for the third time.

It was three months later when I bought the shop. It was a grocery store run by an old couple who were ready to retire.

'This would be great for selling candles,' announced Shelly, who by now, with the help of all the mod cons candlemaking could offer, had graduated from unemployment to selling her candles at a market.

Six o'clock in the morning we would load her ever-more experimental and amazing candles into the back of my van and drive down to build our frosty market stall. By nine o'clock people were looking and she would sell a few here and there. It was like watching Cinderella go to the ball. Something of her was wanted by these people. Something of her was admired by others. She had even quit smoking, and her drinking was dramatically less. I was proud of her, far more so than she would ever be of herself, but I did not love her.

We designed a window for the new shop and called in a signwriter. We painted the shelving and laid floor tiles. We painted the walls and bought in stationery. Shelly set up the shelves with candles, like her own personal art gallery.

The news of the new candle shop spread and she was making a small wage on top of her dole payments and dreamed of one day having a real business. I worked as her shop assistant, just for the involvement, being part of the real world, away from the autism world and my life as an author. We got Monty a new friend, a black collie dog called Charlie, and the two got along so well that they slept together in Charlie's kennel.

Sex was still great, but I felt guilty that I couldn't love Shelly. I needed Margo in the physical world. I needed to hear her voice, to feel her sparkle and be the sister I needed. All I had though were ghosts, of her and of my father, in whose company I felt special. I would spend time just sitting in silence, surrounded by the feel of who they had been, and

Monty would come and sit with me. He seemed to understand where I was.

The insults were just as regular as always, and I felt steeled against Shelly's words whenever she opened her mouth. Then I felt assaulted by her telling me she loved me. She didn't love me, she needed me. She didn't even know me and what she did know she didn't respect. Her dependency was like setting concrete. Her resentment was palpable. Her excuses were hollow and tinny. I didn't love her, but I needed with all my soul to save her as though I were symbolically rescuing the down-and-out girl I'd once been, as though, more to the point, I could rescue my mother, as though, somehow, my background would be a fairytale with a happy ending in which I would one day no longer fear, no longer feel the need to be an exile here ten thousand miles from home.

Shelly was a pie and chips woman and she resented my diet. I stayed off the dairy products and sugar and kept the salicylates low but started to have bread. Progressively I got sicker until the chronic fatigue was back with a vengeance. I began to get viruses which just hung around for ever, until finally I got very very sick.

I had broken out in a rash of oozing sores under my arms and across my stomach. I went to the doctor and it was diagnosed as measles. A journalist who had been for a visit suddenly also became violently ill with measles, as did a woman who visited the shop. I was knocked out. Finally the sores healed and the sickness went. For six weeks the sores were gone. Then, they were back, all of them, back.

'No, they can't be measles,' said the GP looking at them now for a second time. 'Measles doesn't return. You get it, you get over it. You can't get measles again.'

In any case I was seriously ill and went to the pharmacist who asked to see the sores.

'Measles,' she announced.

'Are you sure?' I asked her.

'Absolutely,' she said.

'But this is the second lot,' I went on. 'I had them six weeks ago and now they've come back.'

'That's very unusual,' she said giving me some vitamins to help me cope with the symptoms. 'It's rare, but it does happen very occasionally to susceptible individuals.'

The measles went, and six weeks later they were back again, though fewer. By the end of the year I had had six outbreaks of the same measles virus, each time violently ill. Finally I was almost too weak to drive or keep my hand on the steering wheel. The GP said there was nothing I could do, that I had very few white cells and this often meant it would take longer for someone like me to fight a bug. I phoned a doctor I had heard of who treated Leaky Gut in people with autism-spectrum conditions. I told him I had very few white cells and had caught the measles and seemed to be unable to get rid of them and they were flaring up. He said he could help.

Dr Kenyon was a physician qualified in holistic medicine in which he used a combination of naturopathy and complex homeopathy. He took a medical history. My mother's side of the family had a seventy-five per cent incidence of cancer. My father had died of cancer of the pancreas, liver and bowel. I had a long early history of recurrent ear, nose and throat infections, chronic bronchitis and arthritis prior to dietary intervention several years ago. I also had a previous history of chronic fatigue and bowel problems, severe reactive hypoglycemia and a diagnosis of atypical epilepsy.

He took blood tests for nutrient deficiencies. He took blood tests for my immune system status. He took a saliva swab and sent it off to an Australian lab for genetics testing. The results came back that I had a severe deficiency in magnesium, and a deficiency in essential fatty acids and B vitamins, including B12. My white cell count was low, as we already knew, but my level of inflammatory cytokines – the part of my immune system responsible for inflammatory responses and allergies – was five times the level that would be considered normal. The results of the swab came back. I had a myalgic condition which was inherited and meant that I had an condition in which an inflammation in one part of my body triggered an inflammatory response throughout the rest. My pancreas, liver and gut were all in an inflamed state, and we had to do something to bring this state of red alert back down and get my body working again. Essentially, the measles had triggered this myalgic response and I had M.E. The doctor gave my body a homeopathic dose of what I had to stimulate an immune response, gave me supplements to address the deficiencies and other preparations to help balance blood sugar, help my liver recover and improve my gut function. I paid two hundred pounds and would come back in six weeks. The measles went away.

It was a long hard haul trying to get back into my body. Though I didn't feel physically ill anymore, it seemed I had no stored energy at all and a small amount of exercise was knocking me out.

'You're always tired,' complained Shelly. 'I thought this doctor was meant to sort all this out.'

It took me four months of treatment every six weeks before my energy levels were starting to resemble normal again. I blamed myself for being ill, believing that there was something I could have or should have done to avoid getting ill.

The reprieve had me put all my energies into a new goal. Shelly was sick of our little shop, it didn't bring her enough money to come off the dole. She despaired that she would never get ahead and never have the money to take on a real shop up in the High Street. I told her I would put up the money for the bond and rent in advance, that we could work together to stock it. She shrugged and trundled off to the estate agent only to return in despair, annoyed at me for having raised her hopes. Because she had no financial standing, not even a bank account anymore, and because she was on the dole with no references to prove she'd ever handled such a commitment, they wouldn't even look at giving her a lease, even if she had the money to start.

'Only if I had a guarantor,' she said despairingly.

It was up to me. I could save the kitten or leave it to starve without me. I signed on the dotted line, a ten-year lease. If she didn't pay I would be responsible for the rent on this shop, running or empty, for the next ten years. It was several thousand pounds up front and the rent and rates would come to around twenty-five thousand pounds a year. I had the energy. I could do this. I was the goose that laid the golden eggs.

Shelly was excited, her own shop, a shop in the High Street. She could offer her brother a job. She could invite her mother to help her. She phoned her mother asking her to come down and look at what she had acquired. We dished up a roast dinner for her and her partner and took them down to the shop where they nodded and made suggestions of how they might be able to become part of the business.

Shelly's candles were amazing, and everyone came to admire them. But even those who bought them, didn't burn them. They were simply too nice. There were only so many houses in Malvern and once the novelty of the new shop had worn off, the candles just sat there and the shop started losing money at a furious pace.

The Visa card worked overtime, and Shelly and I went to work to save her business, furiously placing order after order with companies which sold rugs, cushions, incense, essential oils, knick-knacks, lanterns, fountains and wind chimes. We had quickly transformed ourselves into the latest hippie shop in this hippie shop town. Shelly moved to glass painting and our shop overflowed with highly individual bits and pieces. I took to spray painting and produced wild paint effects. Together we had established the shop as 'that place to get something different'. Next came fluorescent coloured twizzlers, metallic dangling streamers, UV lights with buzzy gadgets that spun and twirled and lit up and hypnotized. We sold drums and cymbals, and creatures that giggled when you squeezed them. We sold rolling eyeballs and rubber snakes, clicking frogs and fart whistles. We sold everything we could at rock bottom prices to make it move, but still it was a struggle to pay the rent. By the end of the year we were ten thousand pounds in debt.

Shelly had become captivated by body piercings and looked into becoming a professional piercer. Finally, she would have a profession. She went on a short course and passed. Now she would need a studio. The studio would need plumbing and a toilet, and would have to be completely washable from floor to ceiling. It would cost thousands, and I was the dream merchant. Either I believed in her or I didn't. Either her getting her hopes up, doing this course, achieving anything, was worth something or it wasn't, or she might as well go back to what she had come from. I couldn't sentence her to that. If I did, then somehow it was proof that given the chance I would not have saved my mother from herself either. I phoned the builder. I phoned the plumber.

'What about the equipment?' Shelly asked.

There was an autoclave to buy for sterilizing equipment, there was a proper therapist's couch, there was… Oh, and there was the small matter of having a full selection of the latest gold, silver and titanium body jewellery. We couldn't start off without that.

I kept telling myself it wouldn't matter. I could write another book. What was the point of having money if I couldn't help people? But I felt weighed down, pulled about. And Shelly continued to have moods and throw insults. I continued to go to Dr Kenyon's at two hundred pounds a visit to stay on top of the chronic fatigue as my body recovered slowly. A tax bill came in because of the house I had had to buy the ex-husband. I was running short on available cash. I had to sell something to pay it. Shelly suggested I sell my piano.

The piano gone, I still had some keyboards. They were not worth much but I could still play my music. I sat and wrote a song called 'They':

*They have life in their hands but can't feel it*
*They think it's bought on the street for a quid.*
*They think they left it behind, but that's all in their minds,*
*They think they left it behind as a kid.*

*They have life all around but can't see it*
*They compete and recoil in defeat*
*And they enter all games that society plays*
*And their souls out of reach never meet.*

*Not recently born to it, they're thoroughly bored with it*
*They feel not the magic, they know not the thrill*
*They conform in non-conformity, they live social deformity*
*Appalling in enormity of that delusion they all buy*
*Thinking without it, thinking without it*
*They'd all die.*

Monty wasn't well. He'd been crying in pain when eating his food, and the vet had diagnosed him with gingivitis. He wouldn't be getting better, but we could get all of his teeth out once he was feeling a bit better. He was put on antibiotics.

Shelly couldn't stand the way that Monty smelled. He smelled badly of ammonia where the infection in his gums was rotting his flesh. He climbed onto her lap, she pushed him off. She snuggled with Charlie and I was to take care of 'my' cat.

I gave Monty a cuddle and carried him around before sending him outside with Charlie where his breath would no longer offend.

Monty was depressed, as depressed as I'd ever seen a cat. He seemed to be looking for places to hide. It was strange for him. He was the kind of cat that liked to sit and watch the tennis and TV commercials all day. He used to watch Shelly and me play cards, pacing from one person's hand to the other as though he were reading our hands and having a silent little chuckle about who was winning.

I gave him Rescue Remedy. It was a Bach Flower Remedy recommended for people going through severe depression but it was also given to horses to help carry them in horse floats and it was given to cats and dogs when they were depressed and confused about moving house. The next day Monty was a new cat. Charlie chewed up his ball till it was the size of a golf ball and padded it back and forth gently with old Monty. He began to eat, still wincing with pain but it was no longer as though he had given up hope. By the end of the week he was doing so well I decided this was the time to do it. I'd take him and get his teeth out and we'd get rid of this gingivitis once and for all.

Monty was peaceful and seemed almost happy at the vet's. He purred and accepted the patting from the vet, who took some blood for a blood test. We had to be sure Monty was up to getting the anaesthetic to have his teeth taken out.

A call came in the afternoon, we were asked to come in. Monty wouldn't be having his teeth out. He had cat leukemia. The ammonia smell had not been from the gingivitis. He had kidney failure. He would only live a few more weeks. We could take him home or say goodbye to him here. I snuggled my black hairy friend and told him he was going to go flying the same way Jackie Paper did, the same way Margo did. I told him he would be out of pain and leave his body behind, and that I would miss him but I'd be OK. Then the nurse gave him an injection as he held my hand with his soft black paw, and then Monty had gone too.

Back home, Charlie looked for his friend, pacing about, smelling Monty's old spaces and looking at me and Shelly questioningly. If a dog could have been crying inside, then surely Charlie was shattered. Shelly snuggled with Charlie and we both cried.

'We'll get you another cat,' said Shelly.

I didn't want another cat. Monty wasn't just a cat. He was a person. We had clicked. It seemed that I seemed somehow destined to face ending after ending, as though life were challenging me to confront the beauty and futility of attachment to physical forms which were all, ultimately, transient. I wondered of cat heaven and about cat ghosts. I knew that if I wanted to somehow keep Monty with me, all I had to do was to love the feel of who he always had been and keep that mapped body memory with me in my own lived life. And so now I walked through this challenging time of change with the ghost of my father, of Margo and now of Monty, just as I had spent childhood in the company of my dead grandparents and the characters Carol and Willie. In tribute I wrote Monty a song called called 'Monty's Theme' and played it late into the night.

I had been given the number of a piano player called Jeff. I wanted someone to play my songs professionally and I wanted to sing.

Jeff and I sat down and he played through the chicken scratches I called my sheet music, where I'd tried to teach myself how to write music. He thought they were catchy and he brought them to life like musical magic.

We needed a guitarist and my first thought was Julian, from my days of oblivious homeless wanderings through Europe, a hero in the rain who had once picked me up as a hitchhiking tambourine player, lost in more ways than one.

I called Julian in Germany. He was glad to hear from me; we'd stayed in touch now for nearly ten years. Yes, of course he wanted to come over to Britain for a recording.

It was great to pick up Julian, his ego exuding well beyond the passenger seat to take over the whole car as we drove from the airport to the house.

Shelly was sullen and silent. Julian tried to crack jokes and tell stories in his best English. She was stony and spiky and it was clear he wasn't welcome. After all, he was a man. Shelly felt men smelled bad.

Personally, I liked the smell of men and, aside from Julian's addiction to tobacco, having a man about was a welcome piece of ego over hormones.

'I'm sorry, Donna,' said Julian with his head raised high arriving at the back door, 'but that room you got out there in the backyard it has little creatures. I can't sleep in a room with creatures. I'll just make myself a bed in here. I've got everything I need, me and Charlie can sleep together, don't you think so Charlie?'

Shelly was outraged. Her silence cut me like daggers.

'Oh I wouldn't worry about it,' said Julian on the way to the studio to record our demo with Jeff. 'My wife she does that. I don't pay no attention to it and she takes an aspirin and gets over it. It's nothing.'

Cracks appeared in my lesbian mould and I fell instantly into a crush upon the sound engineer directing me through the glass as I sang. His name was Toby, he was twenty-something, he was utterly self-owning and he had the manner of an angel. Julian sat out in the recording room in between takes and puffed away on his cigarettes, dropping names and crossing and uncrossing his cowboy boots. He and Jeff hit it off like good buddies, and I looked upon the whole scene like a dream I wished would last for ever.

After eight hours we packed up our dream and made ready for home. Julian would be off to the airport the next day leaving Charlie, his new-found love, behind. Jeff said it had been a pleasure, I said a shy goodbye to Toby who had done me the greatest of favours. Perhaps I wasn't a lesbian at all. Perhaps I was simply indiscriminate. Perhaps I was bisexual. Perhaps I just chose human beings and it really didn't matter too much about their gender. Perhaps I was just caught up too much in saving people instead of just being for my own sake. Perhaps one day I would find that.

Shelly decided it was time for me to get over Monty. She didn't understand that he was not simply 'a cat'. He was an entity, a beingness with his own music of beingness, which I knew just as if he was a person. To Shelly it was simply that she had never been close to him. She wanted a cat that was 'our' cat, not 'my' cat. She wanted something that would magically bring out the bonding between us which didn't exist. We went to the cats' home.

We walked along the rows of cats, and she stopped at a cage with a big ginger cat called Crackerjack. It struck out and hissed. Shelly quickly exited the cage locking it behind her and laughing, 'Woah, he IS a Crackerjack.'

'Cheer up,' she said flippantly noticing my sadness at Monty's distinct absence among these cages. 'We're here to get a cat. If you're going to be depressed we might as well go.'

I went from cage to cage patting the fur balls in them, but it only made me sad about Monty no longer having a body and living in the external world.

Shelly had found a cat she liked, Toggles, a playful and exceptionally clingy little 'teenage' cat of six months. The only hitch was that Toggles was one of an inseparable pair. She came with a sister, an all-black sleek little panther called Tomasina. It didn't matter, Shelly decided she would have the other cat too if it meant she could take Toggles. We bought them cat collars and Tomasina went to work biting at the one on Toggles like a possessive mother who felt it didn't belong there.

The last thing I wanted was a cat which at a glance looked so much like Monty but wasn't. And Tomasina, unlike her sister, was completely phobic of social contact and almost feral.

Both cats had been with the cats' home since they were weeks old and had grown up exclusively in the six-foot high, six-foot deep, three-foot wide cage we found them in. This had been the entirety of their six-month-long lives, food on time, toilet in a litter tray and climbing wire. They had worked out roles. Toggles always played the kitten, even leaving her washing up to her sister to take care of, and Tomasina was the surrogate mother.

At home, Toggles burned her whiskers off purring against Shelly's lit candles, pranced upon the stairwell banister and fell off and tried to climb up the walls as she had done in the cage she had lived in all of her life. Tomasina crouched to her belly and slugged her way along the floor in a state of terror and lay huddled and shaking, her hair standing on end. Charlie saw the black cat and came in excitedly waggling his fat curly tail behind. Tomasina lashed out and made a mad dash for the locked cat flap, bashing herself against it over and over till she broke her way through.

The CD was duplicated and even Shelly agreed it was 'alright'. A new friend, Lisa, from down the road, couldn't contain herself. She had played it over and over again, hooked. Shelly conceded to come down to Lisa's and help put the covers onto the demos. I had found a small local shop that was interested in selling them. We would put some up for sale and see how they went. Lisa and I devised a press release, which I sent to the local newspaper with a copy of the demo CD. I got a call. They wanted to do an interview.

It was several months later when the phone rang. It was a journalist from the paper. He had a cutting about the CD. He wanted to meet with me with a view to discussing an article. Was I interested? We could meet at his house if I wanted to.

I arrived at his house, rather nervous. The set-up seemed strange. He greeted me warmly and there was that feeling of ego exuding everywhere, as though Julian might have been hiding in a closet somewhere.

His name was Phil and he offered me tea. I told him I took herbal tea. He asked me into the tiny kitchen to take a look.

There was something about this guy's postures. I felt he was rolling out some kind of a red carpet for me.

He offered me some cold pizza. I explained I couldn't eat dairy products. He ate some himself and began to tell me about himself. He had had manic-depression and was currently diagnosed with M.E. I told him about my own condition. He said he had read about me and thought it might be interesting to meet me. He had had my photo from the newspaper article pinned up at his desk for months and finally got the courage to call.

That I was thirty-six and having a sudden hormone thing as my body decided I wanted to make babies had never occurred to me. All I knew was that somehow I felt captivated by his company, so glad to be indulged when, otherwise, all I felt like was a giving machine. He played psychologist and I played client, answering all of his questions, questions about me, questions about Shelly, questions about being happy. Then I left with a head like cotton wool heading back to Shelly.

I was seeing a hypnotherapist named Natalie. She had good boundaries and blended careful, caring and crazy into a workable recipe. I had gone to see her because I had found myself walking out in front of moving cars and not caring whether I got hit or not. It was always a bad sign. My psychology was fine. I was sensible and you could get nice sane answers out of me. Problem was my emotional state simply did its own thing. I had needed someone who could talk directly to my emotional state, getting around my clever mind. Hypnotherapy with its dream weaving and storytelling did that, and I had found that progressively, without being aware how, Natalie's specially made-up hypnotherapy stories somehow altered my emotional responses to things.

I had told Natalie I was in trouble, that essentially there was not a day I didn't feel on the end of being emotionally abused and used by Shelly. On top of that I had been thinking a lot about whether I would ever have children and I was afraid I wasn't gay after all. She had told me, 'Donna, listen, you are very straight. You come right out and answer everything anyone asks you. You don't have to tell Shelly everything. You can keep some things to yourself.'

So I WAS straight. Natalie had said so. She had said I was straight.

My friend Serge ran a local computer office. He was an eccentric, friendly Frenchman, an art dealer who collected art and also built and supplied computers and taught silly people like me how to use them. Over a lot of hair pulling and tantrums he had taught my very non-techno brain to at least follow the patterns of collecting email and he had created me a website, linking my email to that so that pretty much anybody in the world, or around the corner, could find me.

I had an email. It was from Phil. It was full of emotional tones, tones that he worried about me, tones that he just wanted to make sure I was OK. He finished it off with 'lots of love, Phil' and punctuated the email with a kiss.

I had felt this feeling before. It was when I was thirteen. I had been on a tram late at night travelling back home from my makeshift foster family because my mother had needed me to go to the shops for her. I had been approached by someone with the most wonderful hypnotic voice. I had not understood all of the words but he had said key words which seemed to be buttons. He was from a religious cult called The Children of God and he had looked straight through me. I had felt calm and lulled, and something in me had said jump off the tram and I had run in spite of having no idea what I was running from, but certainly running back to something which held no promises of comfort or family.

My mobile phone had a text message. It was from Phil. He was worried. Could I call him? Then later another. I contacted him to let him know I was fine. He said it was my soul he was worried about. He said he had parked outside my house last night and had almost come to the door to drag me away, out of there. He asked if we could meet. He needed to talk to me. I met with him down at the park and we walked a while before sitting under a tree. He told me I was being used. He just wanted to help me. I needed a friend. There was nothing in this for him.

I listened, certain this stranger in being less subjective had a far clearer perspective on what I was living with than I, myself, had.

He suggested I could run away. I could stay at his place any time I
liked. There wouldn't have to be any sex, though he admitted to finding
me very attractive.

Back home Shelly was depressed. She didn't want to work the next
day. The shop could afford to be closed for a few days. I argued that it
couldn't. You couldn't just leave a High Street shop closed for a few days.
I told her I would take over for a bit.

Phil showed up at the shop and pulled up a stool, greeting customers
like he was part of the furniture.

'Listen,' he told me, 'I'm going down to the coast with my daughter.
She's six and her mother needs a break, so I've got her for the weekend.
It'd be great for you. Say you'll come down. You'll have your own room.
I'll make sure you get food you can eat.'

'I'll ask Shelly,' I said.

I told Shelly that Phil had dropped in. She was steely and glared at
me.

'I know what this guy's up to,' she said with disgust.

'He knows I'm with you,' I said. 'He says he'd like to meet you. Why
don't you meet him.'

She screeched, 'I have no interest in meeting him. I have no interest
in guys. You want to go, you go, but just know what he's after.'

'He says I'd have my own room,' I said.

'Go!' she shouted.

'He says he's just trying to be my friend. His daughter's going to be
there,' I continued.

'Look, do what you like,' she said flatly, 'but I'm not running the
shop.'

'I won't go,' I said.

'Are you interested in this guy?' she asked.

'I have to tell you something,' I replied. 'You'd better sit down.'

Then I told her what my hypnotherapist had said. 'I'm straight.'

There was nothing I could have said that would have closed the
chapter on us as a couple better than that. Shelly left for her mother's
house and I stayed in the house on my own, running the shop by day and
feeding the two cats and the dog we had acquired as a couple.

An email came through. It was from a pair of auties. It was someone called Hal from the original Autism Network International list set up by me, Jim and Kathy all those years ago, together with a guy 'whose life I'd saved', John from LA who had shown up at the Indiana conference I had taken Mick to. They were going to come to visit me.

Hal and John arrived at the station and I brought them to the house. I explained the frosty atmosphere of the house, Shelly's tentative absence, the shop, about Jackie Paper, about Margo and now Monty. I told them about the CD which we played and I told them about Phil. We sat up till the wee hours by candlelight.

John told me how I had saved his life. Hal sat and smiled peacefully like a buddha. They asked me where all my autie friends were. Surely I could call upon them in this state of confusion and chaos I found myself in. I told them I had kept no contacts with the auties who had come and gone in my life over time. John pulled an interesting face and began to flutter his fingers out to the sides. He was checking what he sensed about Shelly, about Phil, about everything, each step in turn.

'You're going to be moving on from here,' he said. 'I can sense it. And this guy Phil... Watch out there, there's nothing there for you. There's something else. You have forgotten your roots, you need to realize your purpose.'

I didn't know any of us had a purpose except to continue to adapt in the face of change. Above all else, I excelled at that.

While they were there, Shelly arrived back. I had moved my things out of 'our room' into a room of my own which I had been struggling to establish for so long. I felt for her. I felt like I was somehow sentencing her to hopelessness. I had promised her nothing, yet my actions had somehow promised her the world. I felt guilty for breathing.

John and Hal paid no attention to Shelly's cold behaviour as she treated them as invisible. By the time they left, the goalposts had shifted and I knew what was needed. Shelly would have to get a flat. It would be damaging to each of us to continue to live together.

Shelly got the paper and by the afternoon had a flat. I agreed to take care of the finances till she got on her feet and off went the furniture all over again.

We agreed that she would continue to run the shop, and there was some unwritten clause which said 'so long as there's still hope for us'. But although I visited her in her flat and stayed over as she settled in, I knew this wasn't going to work.

I sold the house within a week and moved around the corner to a tiny terrace house, taking the animals with me.

The tiny house was a two up, two down, the rooms like little shoeboxes, cramped with even the smallest amount of furniture. It had a kitchen, five foot square including the benches, and just big enough to turn around on the spot. Upstairs were two doorways, one left, one right.

Upstairs, I had been up through the manhole in the ceiling of the bathroom and emerged into a space about five foot long and three foot wide and about three foot high. At the end of this space I spied a hole, a space between two rafters which led into spider-webbed darkness. I was intrigued.

I took a lit candle up there and crawled through the tiny space no more than one and a half feet square. To my surprise, I emerged into a space over the front bedroom, a space ten foot square and eight foot high, a complete other room, untouched, undiscovered, up here in the roof void. I determined it would be a proper room and called Alan, the builder.

Charlie barked all day out in the tiny enclosed garden only big enough for a chihuahua and clung to me whenever I was about, almost afraid even to go to his bowl for fear I would disappear. When he was inside he thundered up and down the stairs, in turn chasing and then being chased by the cats, jumping all over my bed and leaving the bedclothes strewn about as the neighbour complained about 'the noise on the stairs'. One of the cats had taken to peeing everywhere and leaving me presents in the bathtub. Toggles cried from the moment she saw me, seeking to be someone's little baby cat again, and Tomasina behaved as if she were allergic to me. Eventually, Toggles graduated to spending the day crying out in the street, and Tomasina graduated to shitting in her own food bowl. These animals were really depressed. They didn't need me, they needed a new start. We all did. Toggles needed someone to make her special. Charlie needed to live in something other than a terrace house. Tomasina needed psychotherapy.

I took Charlie back to the animal shelter, snugged him and cried as I left him behind to get a real family, one which would last. I pleaded with Shelly to take Toggles back, but she wouldn't have her, and no matter how much attention I tried to show this cat, I was aloof and she was clingy and we didn't click. Phil sent text message after text message to my mobile phone, but there was no way that I needed more confusion on top of what I was already coping with. I stopped returning the calls. I went and bought a ticket. I would take the cats with me. I would return to Australia.

I got a call from Lisa. She was sorry to have to tell me this but the shop had been left closed. Through the letter box came an envelope with a key. Shelly had abandoned the shop just weeks before the Christmas rush, giving up the only chance to recoup some of the large debt that had by now amounted to thirty thousand pounds over the three years. She would be back for the piercing equipment and the jewellery but she was going to make her life somewhere else.

Several days into my running the shop Shelly arrived and took the equipment and the jewellery and her candles. There was no point me having it anyway. I didn't know how to pierce. She told me she had her own plans and I wished her well.

The shelves were full of gaps. Without my funding, Shelly had let things sell and had no money to replace them. I looked for the catalogues. We had to have stock for Christmas. The catalogues were gone. They had been thrown out and I had no idea where to find our stockists. I ordered frantically from every sales representative who walked into the shop and within a week the shop was beginning to shine. Then it hit me. I was guarantor on this place. I would be stuck here for another eight years. There would be no return to Australia. My ticket would have to be cancelled. I wasn't going anywhere.

My cousin Belinda called. She was travelling around the UK and had had no luck getting work. I offered her a job, a car and free rent if she would come up and help me get through Christmas.

Belinda arrived and took over the lounge room, spreading out a camp bed and unpacking the knick-knacks she had collected. She was a bold and outspoken character who could have sold ice to an Eskimo. She started the next day, reorganizing the shop, making signs, chatting to customers as though she'd been in the business all her life.

Toggles and Tomasina welcomed Belinda to the new home, greeting her with cat piss puddles at the foot of the stairs as if to say 'we own this space down here' and brown smelly cat logs in the white bathtub upstairs. Toggles, the tortoiseshell, purred and rubbed and purred and rubbed and clung and cried like someone missing the love of her life, from the moment Belinda walked in. Tomasina treated Belinda the same as she treated me, as though we were worse than the plague.

Belinda had a thing about magic. Everything was a sign. If a number plate had a letter D in it, it was surely a sign telling her to contact her ex, Darren. If she saw a brand name on a product which was the same as Darren's surname, it was a sign reminding her that there was some great mystery she had yet to solve about him. She had an addiction to fortune tellers and Tarot cards and heard that Lisa read them. She had to know what her future held. She had to know if Darren was really Mr Right, if she would ever get back together with him, if this was waiting just around the corner.

We entered Lisa's cluttered Bohemian terrace house. Lisa had Belinda shuffle the Tarot cards and I took a seat on the couch. Lisa looked over at me and gently explained that she did have someone else here in the house, a friend of hers named Chris. She knew I would rather be told, knowing I always took off like a scared rabbit as soon as strangers came into the room.

I stayed for the sake of Belinda's Tarot reading. She waited eagerly to hear what her future held. Then my future came out of the loo and walked down the stairs.

A big hairy leather-clad bloke came ambling down the stairs like Winnie the Pooh, taking a seat next to me on the couch as though this were totally normal.

Lisa introduced Chris, who smiled warmly, and I waited for the panic which didn't come. As those in the room all spoke to each other, something magic did happen. I became swept up in this man's deep chocolate voice, my body attuning to his self-owning movements as he made himself comfortable. There was a boyish shyness to this big warm man, and when he caught my eye and we each looked away, I knew we spoke the same language. I could see in there that however much he was clearly a man, inside of that body was a six-year-old. Far from wanting to escape, I had the compulsion to snuggle up to this stranger. I wanted to smell him, to climb into his arms and be held. He was like a big cloud of peace.

Belinda had had her reading and been told she would need to be patient about Mr Right. It was not what she wanted to hear and so we were off back home. I left the company of the big cloud of peace sitting by me on the sofa and he smiled and waved goodbye, saying it was nice to have met me.

Lisa had a sheepish grin as she walked us out. 'You surprised me,' she said. 'I thought you'd have been straight out when Chris came downstairs.'

'I surprised myself,' I said shyly.

It was a week later, with me and Belinda running the shop, when I could take no more. I phoned Lisa and told her. I had met my Mr Right. He lived just around the corner and up the road. He was too good to let go. I wanted to see him.

Chris arrived in the shop looking about at the fluorescent coloured twizzlers, the shaggy rag rugs, the hanging crystals, the wild lamps. We both found it near impossible to look at each other. Belinda busied herself with the shop in the mayhem of the run-up to Christmas.

Chris gave me a card with his number on it. Lisa had told him. We agreed to go out, and a time and place was set.

At home, Belinda and I scoured his website, pictures of him interspersed with those of his ex. This man did no spring cleaning. I began to get cold feet. What kind of a man breaks up with his ex and continues to live with her? And what the hell was all this Pagan, Goth, Geek thing?

Chris arrived at my little rabbit warren of a house, his long hair tied back in a pony tail. All doubt melted. I directed him to the car and we drove into Worcester.

On either side of the table, we went together like salt and pepper. He ordered what he wanted. I ordered what I could. He asked me about the shop, and I told him about Shelly. He told me about his ex, how they had broken up six months ago after she had decided she needed to sleep with other people and how he hadn't got around to telling her to move out yet. This was something I had never encountered. A male doormat. A big, leather-clad, hairy male doormat. I asked him about all the labels and he shrugged his big shoulders. I explained that labels were inevitable but I tried to avoid letting them stick, because otherwise you tend to try to be loyal to them when you would otherwise maybe be free to outgrow them.

I was lost in his chocolate voice. He was swept up in the gentle rhythm of mine.

Chris was like Pooh Bear, he lived in the moment, plodding along yet easy and playful like a breeze. It was as though he was unable to accumulate resentment or form social judgements even though his obsession with the news and teletext meant he was right up to date with the news and could argue political opinions.

His nature attracted people who all found him so 'nice', 'sweet', 'kind', yet he had been so playfully shy until his twenties that he had been cripplingly lonely, finding it difficult to converse and mostly unable to build friendships. We suited each other like tea and biscuits, and he didn't mind at all that I swung between nervously being compelled to dominate the conversion and slipping back into silence. In fact, he had such a silent cheeriness, it was as if the silence itself was full of company.

We went out walking in the cobblestone streets, surrounded by darkness and city lights. We agreed to head up to the hills.

It was pitch black when we turned off the car lights and we had to feel our way up the hill. It was bitey cold in the December wind, and my skirt blew all around me as I clambered up the hill, stumbling in the dark. Only a hint of moonlight illuminated a rock here or there, and Chris offered me a hand as we climbed. I took it and we giggled, the wind trying to blow us about like leaves.

At the top, we stood on a saddleback ridge, the city lights emerging and twinkling in the distance below. Chris stretched, breathing in the crisp night air. Then he lay on the frosty ground looking up at me and at the stars. He reached upward with a hand and I took it, climbing down onto him. Then I kissed him. He stroked my hair and said 'I didn't mean for you to do that. I mean, I didn't expect you to do that.'

'I know,' I said, smiling to myself. I lay down on the frozen ground next to him, nestling in the curve of his arm as I had so wanted to at Lisa's house that night I had met him. We lay quiet and easy in each other's company, looking up at the stars.

The frost told us it was time to go, and we climbed down the hill to the car, feeling our way in the dark. I drove Chris to his house and dropped him at the foot of the hill, leaving him to make his way up to the door where his ex was up with the light on.

I went home in a strange state. It was weird to drop this man off to a house with another woman. It didn't feel right. But until that moment, all had been like a fairytale. Mick, who had come to finally dislodge my pain of being in love with the Welshman had now, with much relief, become 'Mick who?'.

I drifted through the door, met by Belinda eager to hear all about my evening. I wanted to keep hold of the feeling, to keep it just mine, but I chattered about Chris and shared my reservations about this business of him living with his ex.

'It's just not natural,' said Belinda. 'He's a nice guy, there's no doubting that, but he must be weak or something. Why didn't he just tell her to piss off?'

It was a good question. When a phase of life ends, you clear up the debris ready to move on, clear boundaries, no muddy water. I really didn't need the chaos of falling in love with a man who had one foot in the past.

'You ought to give him a chance,' Belinda went on. 'A lot of blokes just don't know how to end things. He'll probably sort it out now he's going out with you.'

I wanted to be the princess in the castle, the one he came home to. I certainly didn't like the logical conclusion that if I developed a relationship with this guy one day I would be the one waiting home with the light on whilst someone else dropped my fella off, ex or not. In the homeless domestic prostitution of my teens, I had been that. I had been a doormat to a womaniser. There was no way I wanted in with that kind of drama.

It wasn't long before Chris came into the shop. He had some friends coming over to his house who had been visiting Australia. Would I like to come around to his house?

The thought of meeting his ex was daunting to say the least, but I took up the offer. She couldn't be too bad if she was fine about me visiting.

'What!' exclaimed Belinda. 'You're going to meet the ex?'

I clarified that I was going around to meet Chris's friends and that, yes, she would happen to be there. She wished me luck.

It was evening and I had closed up the shop, and having been briefed by the worldly-wise Belinda I drove around to Chris's house up on the hill. The lights twinkled in the distance, and it felt safe out here as I climbed the hill to his house. I knocked at the door.

Chris answered and I entered the lounge room. At the other end of the room, facing the door, was a young woman on a rocking chair, rocking back and forth expectantly, dressed in the typical 'Pagan', 'Goth' garb. She slid a silver chalice towards me across the wooden table, her face suppressing a smile to herself, her eyes fixed like an animal about to catch its prey.

'Here, have a wine,' she said, looking from me to Chris, to Chris's guests expectantly, as if taking the chalice were some kind of test.

I picked it up. It was red wine, high in salicylates, I would be out of it by the end of the glass.

'You don't have to drink it,' said Chris.

I sat myself on the floor and Chris took a place next to me. The young woman continued rocking, bringing up Chris's nicknames and all the reasons for them, highlighting her intimate knowledge of him as though marking territory for my sake.

She discussed men and their physiques, referring to Hollywood action films like a connoisseur and getting consensus from the guests with tittering laughter. Chris said hardly a word. The guests seemed dominated by her as she led the course of the conversation.

The conversation turned to how she was a reincarnated spirit of a Native American Indian, how her great-grandfather had become blood brothers with an indigenous person of the Americas and how she was going to get a tattoo, ivy running down the length of her back.

'You should get a tattoo too,' she said turning haughtily to me. 'I know... A snake, that'd suit you.'

Chris whispered that perhaps we shouldn't sit together. He didn't want to upset his ex. I lost the plot.

'I can't believe you said that,' I said, scurrying backwards along the carpet as though he had turned into some monster and getting to my feet.

'Don't be like that. Don't be like that,' pleaded Chris in a whisper. 'I didn't mean it.'

'I'm sorry,' I said. 'This isn't my thing. I'm out of here.'

'Let me come with you,' said Chris. 'Please.'

'Suit yourself,' I said, leaving.

I let myself out and Chris hurried after me standing by my car window like a lost sheep.

'Please, can I come to your house,' he pleaded. 'I don't feel right here. I don't feel like staying in that house.'

'That's your own house,' I said incredulously.

'I know,' he said shaking his head in despair as the drizzle swept around us.

I let him into the car.

Chris was crying like some big rain clouds had broken in his soul. I listened and he explained that he hadn't known what to do when she'd announced to him that she wasn't interested in him anymore. He knew he should have asked her to leave then but didn't know how a person does that. So he had stayed, gone on antidepressants and waited for her to show him where this big mess went. Then he had watched as she made her interests known to his closest friends, whilst he continued to pay the bills and keep a roof over both of their heads. Tonight, he realized, their amicable agreement was not going to work, at least not on his part.

We sat up till late and finally came the question of going to bed. He asked if he could stay. He didn't want to go back there. He didn't want to go back there until she was out.

I took Chris by the hand and we went upstairs to my room. He sat on the side of the bed taking off his boots.

'I'm not expecting anything,' said Chris, trying to let me know he wasn't hitting on me.

'I might be,' I said with a cheeky look.

'If things don't work out between us,' he said, 'I would want to know you would always want to stay friends with me'.

'No way,' I said bluntly. 'If I sleep with you and it doesn't work out, I believe in clear boundaries. I couldn't go from that to being friends. Friends is friends, lovers is lovers.'

Chris took off his boots, his socks, his T-shirt, his trousers, his boxer shorts, and climbed into my bed and turned his back to me. He was such a strange man, such a boy in this thirty-year-old body.

I put my arm around him, smelling his male smell, smelling his hair. I felt the hair on his body. He snuggled close in to my body, holding my hand like a child in the dark. I put my face to his shoulder and he turned around to face me in the semi-darkness, his face moist from tears. He wrapped me up in those big arms, pulled me in towards that hairy body and held me tightly. My body was electric, and I hoped finally to succeed with Chris where I had failed with Mick and with the Welshman. To feel like a whole woman with a man, in charge of my own sexuality, able to take what I wanted.

I indulged in Chris's body like an artist set loose with paint on a canvas. I indulged like a frustrated virgin, a teenager eager to know, yet sensual as if I were swimming in the depths of this beauty of closeness. Then I held him, breathless and overwhelmed, my body shaking, as did his. I smiled and stroked his long black hair which fell around me as he nuzzled up to me.

'Lovers,' I said.

'Lovers,' said Chris with a tangible innocence.

The next day, I devoured Chris all over again but couldn't eat my breakfast. It was as though the Exposure Anxiety was popping out everywhere to compensate for the huge freedom I had won.

'You want to get a breakfast?' asked Chris.

'I'm just got to finish this,' I replied, lacquering the bathroom floor with varnish and painting myself into a tiny square.

'Come on, leave that and come for a breakfast,' cajoled Chris.

'I can't,' I said, honestly.

Chris was learning about Exposure Anxiety.

At the foot of the stairs the cats had left him a present. Together we cleaned up the mess.

That evening, Chris arranged to meet with some friends. He couldn't tell his ex himself, so he had asked these friends to intervene and tell her on his behalf.

The phone rang, it was his ex. Chris and I left.

His ex arrived at the house and the friends sat her down. They told her enough was enough. What she was doing to Chris was wrong and she would have to move on and she could always move back in with her mother.

I received an email. It was from his ex, then another, then another. The emails were inviting me to discuss with her the need for her to move out of Chris's house. Didn't I realise she had nowhere else to go? Didn't I understand she couldn't work because she was a highly sensitive person and the world out there would drive her straight into a lunatic asylum? All were signed 'in love and respect' and finished with her adopted Native American Indian name.

This wasn't my responsibility. Why was it that such so-called 'found' people were so often utterly 'lost'? I had my own problems.

Chris hadn't gone home and I hadn't minded at all. But he had unfinished business back there. His ex was not budging. If he wanted her out he would have to tell her, not ask her, and he would have to do it himself.

Chris walked from his work to the shop and stayed with me as I turned out the lights on the day's chaos. I dropped him around at his house. He said he would call when he was ready to be picked up. He climbed the hill.

Inside, his ex was already waiting for the visit. She had a bottle of wine sitting ready on the table. She had decided to move on. She would go live with her mother.

Chris called, he was ready to come back. He had a date for her departure. He would provide her a reference as a tenant in case she ever needed it. She would leave in two weeks. His house would be free the day after Christmas.

I settled into the idea that Chris would be staying with me for the next two weeks and that he wanted to spend Christmas with us, me and Belinda.

'Listen it's alright for you two,' said Belinda crossly, 'stuck to each other like fly paper or something. But in case you haven't noticed, I haven't got a boyfriend and it's very uncomfortable with you two always hanging off each other everywhere I go. Do you think you might hold back a little?'

Chris and I scurried up the stairs like a pair of children and wrapped Christmas presents. We had a wicker Christmas tree and wanted a real Christmas. The room next door was in chaos from the building work to recover the discovered room up in the roof. We tacked up a big colourful throw to create a nice-looking wall over the chaos and dragged the dinning table upstairs. We set up the wicker tree and decorated it. We put the presents under the tree.

At the shop it was chaos, as Belinda and I tried to keep the shelves full and the customers happy. It was a wonderful time, and although the shop had a huge debt behind it, I enjoyed the structure and the fact that nobody could sack me, no matter whether I got it right or wrong. Not like last year, when the window got set on fire because of all the cotton wool in the window and Santa went up in flames. This year, Belinda was the brains of the operation and kept the place ticking. The newly arrived Aussie was popular with the local people, and they talked to her about Australia and how she was coping with the English winter and whether she liked it here. I had cancelled my own ticket back when I had been left with the shop, but having met Chris that all felt right now.

Chris came and worked with us on Saturdays, putting goods into bags for people, wrapping people's presents, making herbal tea. Finally, we closed, the day before Christmas day, bolted the door after the last customer around nine in the evening, and all collapsed in a heap with a sigh of celebration. We had made it, the shelves looked bare and ransacked, the counter was in a state, the window had been stripped of stock as it sold straight out of the window, and this motley crew had held this sinking ship together all the way till Christmas.

The next day, Chris and I woke up to the smell of roast dinner coming from the kitchen where Belinda was cooking. She chastised us for leaving it up to her, and we did our best to pitch in and help. We had set a table in our makeshift dining room with its hidden building works, its recycled 1970s glass-top table and a curtain for a tablecloth. Together with Belinda, we pulled Christmas crackers, unwrapped presents and ate dinner by candlelight. It was wonderful. Even the cats gave us a break for a change with no pee to have to clean up.

On Boxing Day we sat about rather quietly, knowing Chris's ex was moving out of his house. Now he would be going home.

Chris asked if I would come back with him to his now vacant house. It was strange to wander about now it was just his house, a two-up, two-down house like mine was but with slightly larger rooms. He was reasonably tidy as far as blokes go, with a great love of books, shelves and shelves of them, books on history, archaeology, physics and foreign cultures and their religions, myths and rituals, books on speaking Welsh. He had ordnance survey maps showing all the hidden footpaths throughout rural England and Wales, and castles, burial mounds and ruins.

There was a book on Attention Deficit Disorder. Chris explained that he had problems staying on a task and thought he had a very poor memory. The only exception was the way he worked with computers, where he could barely keep himself away from them.

The place was thick with dust, the kitchen floor as though it had never had a clean, the window sills sticky from dirty mugs and dust. I asked for a cloth and started to scrub. Chris began to cry. He had been working too hard to get around to doing these things; he was touched that someone would want to on his behalf. I knew that with all the dust and gunge out of the way, my allergic state was not so likely to be aggravated. But more than this, the place felt unloved and I felt sad about that. I felt he was a worthy man, a man worthy of a clean house, a proud house. Besides, it was no drama to me. I felt at home when I had a purpose and I loved any job that was systematic and linear in its progression. Cleaning was like that, one big progressive path throughout the entire house.

He fetched some coal from the garage at the end of the row of houses and lit an open fire. Then he ordered us some Chinese food with no MSG.

'Would you like to watch a video with me?' asked Chris.

'OK,' I replied.

He fetched out *The Princess Bride*, a fantasy film and comedy. The Chinese food arrived. He was a homemaker. This felt like home.

It got dark, then it got late.

'Would you like to stay?' asked Chris. 'I'd like it if you'd like to stay here with me.'

He sounded like such a boy and so alone.

'I have to have special food,' I replied, referring to my dietary wheelchair which was part of my daily stability. 'I've got to take supplements.'

'I've got food,' said Chris.

'No,' I replied. 'I've got special food, Rice Milk, dairy-free margarine, food that has no sugar and is low in salicylates.'

'I've got Ribena,' said Chris. 'Is that any good?'

'Only if I want to be off my head,' I replied gently.

'Could we go and pick up your food and come back?' he asked.

The man was a sweetheart. He appeared to take my diet and regime as completely normal and no imposition at all.

'I've got Chinese food for tonight. We could go to my place first thing in the morning,' I replied. 'I've got to feed the cats.'

I felt good in Chris's house, with his warm hospitality, with his music and a lounge room, with his books I would never read, and the feeling that my man had his own house and I was being welcomed into it.

I decided to start up the consultancy again. Belinda and I would run the shop as a gift shop and stock everything which could make an Autie buzz. We had drums and chimes and musical instruments, fabrics of all kinds, things which spun and whirled, things which caught the light and things to flick. I would run the consultancy from what had once been the body piercing studio.

Belinda and I set about creating a flyer for the new consultancy until we were happy with it, then we gathered a mailing list and sent it out. The phone started ringing.

People loved the changes to the shop and asked what the theory was behind the unusual collection of objects we stocked. I explained that I wanted to remind people of the child within themselves, that it was safe to buzz, to play, to be silly and let go, and that maybe, somewhere in there, they would better understand the sensory highs and fascinations of many people with autism. Then in consultancy I bridged the divide from the other side. I tested children for the use of more affordable BPI tinted lenses to reduce light frequencies so they had more time to keep up with other incoming information. I advised parents about how to interact with someone with Exposure Anxiety. I designed language programmes to help children who couldn't link concepts with the sounds of words. I set about advising parents about dietary interventions and talked about the cocaine-like highs caused by salicylate intolerance, the opiate-like effects of dairy and gluten intolerance, and how to reduce the drunkenness caused by candida in children with Leaky Gut. My kids progressively began to shine. Some who didn't speak began to verbalize. Some who couldn't understand began to keep up better. Some who had been bouncing off the walls were able to control themselves. Some who had been caught up in a cycle of involuntary self-protection mechanisms had been able to let down their guard and explore. Children became toilet trained.

So your child will only use a nappy and not the toilet? And you are waiting ready to praise when he uses the toilet? And he avoids praise and attention when you initiate? Then be nonchalant about the toilet and show off about the nappy.

Your child is eating pebbles and the more you say no the more it compels the child to eat pebbles? Then say yes and chase the child enthusiastically with pebbles too large for its mouth. It'll soon be forced to counter your enthusiasm by losing interest in eating the pebbles.

My strategies were surreal but they made sense of each child's individual social-emotional take on the world, their way of perceiving and their personality, and they often worked.

Belinda was leaving. The shop didn't earn enough to pay her what she deserved and she had made up her mind to leave this cold country and return to Australia a little wiser than when she left. She said goodbye to the cats, to me and to Chris, and caught the train to London and to go home. I thanked her for her help and for being the reason I had met Chris. She wished us well and headed back to Australia.

I had an appointment with the estate agent for the shop. I explained the situation, how I had signed as guarantor but had truly believed Shelly would not have left me lumbered with a shop. I was told tough luck. I had several options. I could run the shop for the next eight years, losses or not. I could close the shop and simply fork out for the rent and rates on an empty shop for the next eight years. Finally, I could buy my way out. The owner suggested that eight thousand pounds would be acceptable under the circumstances to let go of the contract.

I decided to buy my way out of the contract. Chris and I, together with Lisa, drew up signs for a closing down sale that Saturday and waited for the vultures to pick our bare bones.

It was madness, like it had been at Christmas, and by the end there were only enough things to fill a few boxes. We sat about on the floor and celebrated freedom with chips. Then we cleaned everything away, whitewashed all the walls and I handed back the keys and a cheque for eight thousand pounds.

With Belinda gone, Chris spent more time back with me at my house as we lived between two houses. Finally, it was decided that he would put his house up for rent and live here with me and the cats. We went to war with the never-ending toilet on the carpet routine and turds in the bath.

We tried everything: tin foil on the floor, crushed garlic, even taking up the carpet entirely, but nothing would help. On top of that Toggles was still pining for Shelly, and Tomasina was no less allergic to people than she ever was. Finally, came the last straw. Toggles took a pee as bold as day as we sat in the dining room then ran off. Together we decided we had had it. Toggles needed to go and besides it would do her sister good if she was to be separated from her. She needed a chance at a new home, a new start where she could be the only cat in a family. This would give Tomasina a chance to turn towards people and not cringe and run in fear every time a human being walked by.

I had helped my neighbour face her own cat dramas, and now, in her strong solid boundaries, she came to my aid. We drove Toggles to the cats' home and handed her in. I felt so sad for her but I knew her heart was already broken and only a change, a complete change, would have the chance to fix it. I went home to Tomasina, and after three days of crying and searching for her sister she came and purred around our legs and climbed up onto our laps, deciding that humans weren't so bad after all. Then, just as we thought our days of cleaning cat pee were over, she did the same as her sister and, bold as day, took a pee in the dining room right in front of us.

I continued running the consultancy, discussing things like toilet training and behavioral problems and couldn't even master these problems with my own cat. I began to get ill again, catching every bug that walked through my door, struggling to get over them until it was like I just had one big long cold. I kept booking time out and driving down the country to see Dr Kenyon. Finally, he took a live blood sample and we looked at it. As we already knew from earlier blood tests, there were very few white cells, essentially no immunity. But what we saw alarmed me now because the live blood, which was meant to be able to flow about, sat glugged together, tightly compressed, the surface of the blood cells spiky where they should be smooth.

'What's that?' I asked.

'Mycoplasma, most likely,' said Dr Kenyon. 'It's bacteria which shouldn't be there, it makes the cell walls spiky like that so they don't transport nutrients and oxygen like they should. And see there,' he pointed to one of the few white cells, 'see it's inactive and all hairy like that. It's infected. That's why your body isn't fighting anything. This is pretty bad. It's everywhere.'

'Isn't that what happens with cancer?' I asked. 'Where the body gets sick and too tired and toxins and bugs just take over.'

'Yes,' said Dr Kenyon. 'And with your family history, we don't want that.'

'How did all this bacteria get there?' I asked.

'Some of the damage here is from gut bacteria that have crossed into the bloodstream because of Leaky Gut,' said Dr Kenyon. 'Basically you don't have any gut immunity. All that bacteria getting into your blood is what's sending your neurotransmitters haywire up in your brain, and why you've got high levels of that naughty quinolinic acid up showing up in your urine analysis. Some of this sticking together of all the blood cells is caused by oxidative stress; the chronic anxiety is going to make that much worse, especially with an inflammatory state like you've got. Thing is, what to do about it?'

'I just want to clean my blood up,' I replied.

'Yes, we both do,' said Dr Kenyon.

He put me on a supplement called a transfer factor which was used with people with immune deficiency. It cost a fortune, and together with Dr Kenyon's fees, I was basically working to pay for my health.

I had the man of my dreams but I didn't have my health. If I could get that then, on the right diet, with a healthy immune system, then one day he and I might have a child together, a family of my own, a new start and a way of feeling not so bad about my own background.

I had always been put off by the idea, mostly because sexuality had been such a struggle, but also because the constant shutdowns and wild chaotic chemistry had made life such a struggle that I would not have wished my state on my worst enemy. Since diet and Glutamine, most of that was taken care of, it was just a matter of the Exposure Anxiety. Still, every day, it was impossible to get me to eat because I was having involuntary avoidance, diversion and retaliation responses in relation to the expectation to eat food. As soon as I knew breakfast time was expected, I was anywhere else but there. When the food was put out, I instantly felt claustrophobic, suffocated, desperate to get the food away from me and back in the cupboard. I had talked to Chris about playing hard to get and he had become a master of flippantly announcing he was off to breakfast and he would see me later, words which had me drop what I was doing and race him down there, compelled not to be the one abandoned and left behind. He would serve up the smallest of servings to provoke me into feeling starved so I'd go for more. He would put out a teaspoon so I'd feel less force-fed and not give up after the first spoonful.

Getting a coat, using the toilet, putting on shoes, getting a drink, going out ... for all of these activities we had to use strategies to outwit this out-of-control, redundant so-called 'self-protection' mechanism. Chris would come home only to find that this Exposure Anxiety would have me in tears, having held on for the toilet for hours, unable to get a drink or have my lunch, or having been cold all day, unable to initiate and follow through the simple act of going to get a jumper and putting it on.

But hormones had me, and Chris would have made such a wonderful father that I found myself wishing that one day Exposure Anxiety would be out of the way too, and that it was not yet too late to think about having a child.

Then I ended up at the doctor's. An ultrasound scan had found a large cyst growing inside one of my ovaries, over on the right. I would have to have surgery.

Chris and I cried together in the park over lunch. I was terrified of hospitals, and even more scared knowing I would likely not have any immunity to all the bugs I would be exposed to there. I was scheduled for an operation in a few weeks. It was to be simple keyhole surgery. They would go in through my belly button, drain the cyst, and let me go home the next day.

In the weeks that followed, we distracted ourselves by buying a house where two people could stand in the kitchen at the same time. We would leave this wonderful little shoebox and move to a bigger house with its own garden and no foreign cats outside waiting for our phobic Tomasina. Perhaps it would be the start she needed. Perhaps we would conquer the never-ending saga of the toileting problem.

We would miss this little house but it was really a one-person place. We would miss our newly found neighbours in the terrace and the communal feel to the place. We would miss the walks at the end of the street where crowded suburbia suddenly finished along a long, grassy lane down to the stream. But we would have a real kitchen and a lounge room you could dance about in, and a view of sunsets far across the Malvern Hills, and I would have an office right underneath the house in the flat which came along with it. We would take a mortgage on the shoebox and rent it out. The new house would be ours in six weeks.

The day arrived for the surgery and Chris took time off work to come with me. I told them about hypoglycemic attacks so they knew to watch out for them. I was wheeled into the operating room, given anaesthetic through a needle in the back of my hand and they went to work.

I awoke out in the recovery room, pleased it was over. The doctor had to come and see me, then I could go home.

The doctor arrived. He told me he had bad news. They had gone in to drain the ovary over on the right and realized it was not the right-hand ovary. It was the left-hand one which had travelled over to the right along with a severely damaged tube which had become inflamed and distended and attached itself to my other organs. In short, it was a mess in there. I needed to come back. I was asked if I ever wanted to have children and told that the best way to take care of the mess in there was to remove all of my reproductive organs. I was scared as hell.

'Is this cancer?' I asked.

'We don't know,' said the doctor. 'It's very unusual. We could probably save the right-hand side which seems intact,' he went on, 'but everything from the left-hand side has spread everywhere and attached itself to everything. It's all very inflamed. We need to get all of that out. This is a big operation. You'll have to have a cut across your tummy.' He pointed out the six-inch line he'd need to cut.

'If I can keep any of my insides, I want to keep them,' I told him. 'But take out what you need to take out.'

I asked when I would have to come back. He told me he had scheduled me back in just before my birthday.

Chris was scared. He had just found the love of his life and now she was in big trouble. We were trying to stay calm, but we were both really shaken up with so little time to think. He treated me like a princess, snuggled up with me and read stories to me, made me cups of herbal tea and cooked Donna-safe dinners. I looked at this man and his warmth. He was everything I would ever have needed in a parent. With a simultaneous sense of self and other, with body connectedness, with an absence of total shutdowns and Exposure Anxiety that was at least much less than it ever used to be, I was the child I wished I had been.

'Did you ever want to have kids?' I asked.

'Never really thought about it,' said Chris. 'Did you?'

'Most of my life I was certain I never wanted to,' I said. 'The thought of someone clinging, following me about, needing me. I used to get so claustrophobic I thought for sure I'd have locked myself in a cupboard. But I've thought about it. You'd have made a great father.'

'Oh, that's lovely,' said Chris. 'Thank you. But I wouldn't miss it if I was never a father.'

'If I'd ever had a child, I'd have wished it was with you,' I told him.

'This is our family,' said Chris pointing at himself and then at me. 'This is enough for me.'

'I don't know what will happen if they have to take everything out,' I said quietly.

'Well, all I care about is that they return you back to me,' said Chris.

'Without my gubbins?' I asked referring to my soon-to-be-absent body parts.

'If that's what brings you home healthy,' said Chris. 'You'd still be the same you. Nothing's going to change there.'

'You wouldn't miss having children?' I asked.

'Nope,' said Chris. 'You and I are pretty much still children.'

Some people make errors of judgement and choose the wrong people. Some people have such a lack of judgement that they fail to tell the wrong people to piss off. Some people have a bit of both, and if they ever get anything right it is a miracle or an accident or that roll of the dice some call Destiny. Whatever that was, I had got something right and I knew it totally. I knew it in my bones. It wasn't a knowing in my head. It wasn't like getting carried away with an idea. It was like a feeling of recognition, like when you come to an understanding about God. I had come to that understanding about Chris.

I phoned up the restaurant we had gone out to on our first date. I went and bought a card and a candle and some matches. I told Chris I wanted him to come out with me.

'Why?' he asked. 'What's this all about?'

I refused to answer.

I wore the clothes I had worn when he first went out with me. We had been going out together six months by now. It was midsummer solstice but still chilly, and I wore my long dark coat, the one Jean had given me. In the pocket I had the card, the candle and the matches.

All through dinner, I kept staring at this man, unable to give him the card. It was a wonderful time and we laughed and I felt warm like toast in his company.

I seized my last chance.

'Can we go up the hills?' I asked.

We headed for the hills and arrived not far from where we had clambered up the hill that night. It was dusk and the sky was dim with a wind that danced around us as we climbed the hill, this time ever so carefully together taking small steps. We arrived at a bench seat in front of a large tree with a panoramic view of the hills beyond. Chris and I sat down.

I reached into my pocket. It wasn't so dark yet that I would need the candle or the matches. I brought out the card with my letter in it. I handed it silently to Chris. He smiled to himself and opened the envelope taking out the card. It was a white lace-edged card with a single red rose on it. He opened out the letter which was inside it and read:

*My Dearest Chris,*

*I wanted to say something important to you.*

*I love you like you are family to me, you are my best friend, my lover, my partner.*

*I am proud of you and proud to be part of watching you become ever more confident and aware. I'm honoured to be there for you. I feel supported in how you are there for me. I know with all my heart that you are a good man and that your love for me is rock solid. I know we are strong as a couple and absolutely committed to our relationship as the most valuable of things in our time together. I trust our connection is one in which I can grow and feel acceptance no matter what comes my way and I love so very much to give you the same feeling. I trust you will always respect my individuality but never so blindly that I would doubt my equal respect for your own and I trust that I want just you and that it will stay so for me.*

*So knowing all this, I would like to say that I've changed my view about being married, Mr Samuel. I would feel privileged if you were to marry me. So, as it's a leap-year, I am daring on this special midsummer's night to ask if you would like to be married ... To me.*

*In the hills, among the trees, swinging from the trees ... I don't mind. I just feel that this is one thing I want with you ... Mr Samuel. Marry me?*

*Love from your special woman ...*

*Donna XXX*

Chris was silent, a glimmer in his eyes, his face breaking into a smile as he folded the letter.

'Yes,' he said. 'The answer's yes.'

Then as if they'd been waiting in the silence, a flock of birds suddenly rose out of the tree in front of us and flew high up into the air and away across the hills as we drew our breath in awe.

The contracts were signed and we filled up the truck with our things, me being careful not to lift much. The people moving into the shoebox helped us move our stuff out and Chris's friend Leo came around to help. Off we went to the new house. That evening we watched the sun set in a panoramic view from our back window.

Tomasina settled in like a star, and even used the cat flap. She was brave, especially with a dose of Rescue Remedy, even though she raced back in, her hair all standing on end, because of some drama in her little cat head none of us could fathom. Then one day she came in with an old cat collar which became her best friend, and she chased it, threw it in the air and slept with it as though it were part of her sister she had discovered. In the process, Tomasina finally broke out of her own autistic shell and we saw the kitten in the cat for the first time.

The date for the operation came around. I had been following Dr Kenyon's advice regarding the supplements and trying to boost my immunity in order to cope. He'd sent me a few more things to help me recover after the operation and I felt armed.

Chris took time off work and stayed with me as I changed into a very non-me hospital gown and laid myself down on the very non-me bed. I felt eaten up by the foreignness; panic gripped my stomach and chest and a scream rose in my throat. I felt trapped in here. We did some deep breathing. Chris put my monkey on the bed, Mr McGibbon.

The doctor arrived, and Chris kissed me goodbye as I was wheeled off on the operating table.

'See you when you come back out,' he said cheerily. 'We're waiting.'

The surgeon inserted the needle and delivered the anaesthetic. My body was in tremors, as though it knew what was coming.

I awoke with Mr McGibbon and Chris sitting next to the bed. I was connected up to all kinds of tubes and bottles as though my body was no longer mine but part of a factory.

There were other beds around me with women in them, all in non-me gowns like mine, some hooked up to equipment, others able to move around. I double-checked where everything was. I could hardly move, and to move caused great pain. I snuggled Mr McGibbon.

They had taken out the damaged ovary and the fallopian tube which had grown all over the place in there. They had detached it from where it had connected itself with scar tissue to other organs, including my bowel. They had left my right-hand ovary and tube intact, healthy and functioning.

The doctor arrived and I had asked him about cancer. They would do some tests on what they had removed. For some reason, the tube had grown many times its usual length, taking over. It had not been an infection as the right-hand tube and ovary were in good health. It looked like some kind of inflammatory condition.

The next day, I noticed my visual perception was much better. For months I had had to wear the more deeply tinted of my BPI tinted lenses to try to hold visual cohesion together, without which I was far more meaning blind and context blind. Now I was able to wear the almost clear ones. There were conversations all around me among patients; without meaning to, I mapped their conversations, their words tumbling about in my head in spite of trying to let them go. Conversations about hysterectomies, ectopic pregnancies, about miscarriages and who had developed secondary hospital infections.

I had to get out of there. I had to get all these tubes and needles out of me. I wanted to go home.

I had a six-inch cut across my abdomen and had staples to hold my flesh together. I was hooked up to catheters, a drain removing blood from any internal bleeding and a drip delivering nutrients. I began to panic. I just needed to get to a quiet space, somewhere dark and alone with no noise and no people. In great pain, I made my way off the bed, wheeling the medical paraphernalia with me, hyperventilating and crying. A nurse stopped me as I headed out of the ward inch by inch, wincing in pain with each jolting step. I managed to utter that I was a person with autism and it had all got too much, that I needed to get away, I needed somewhere silent and dark and small. She led me to a cleaner's room with little more than a few mops and buckets and got me a chair. Then she left me alone, waiting just outside the door.

I gave myself a rhythm, humming a tune to myself as I went and trying to breathe properly. Finally, I emerged, tears now streaming silently, I made my way back to my bed and got back in.

Chris arrived and brought along some food which I could eat. I wanted just to be taken home and it was so hard for him because I had to stay at least five more days. He held my hand and sang little songs and talked to me via McGibbon. Finally, I promised to try my hardest to stay just one more day, one day at a time.

I lasted three days before I panicked and pulled out my drip. I had asked for them to take the needle out of the back of my hand. It had been distressing me, a sign of my imprisonment. Finally, the compulsion to just free myself from it momentarily became overwhelming and I pulled it out. Then, immediately, the panic set in. I was in trouble. Blood wanted to come spurting out. I held my thumb tightly over the entry point and whispered ashamedly for help. I explained I couldn't help it, that I felt claustrophobic and it just overtook me. I went painfully back to the cleaner's room and sat on a chair.

When Chris arrived that evening, I insisted that today I was going home, staples and all. The staff warned against it but finally gave in and allowed me to go home under the care of Chris's parents who had come to help out and run the house for me. I was to have a home nurse who would come around and check on me but I was going home.

The trip home was like being released from a prison. I didn't care if I had to stay in bed for a month, as long as it was my bed with my sheets and familiar noises around me.

The nurse finally removed the staples, giving me strict orders to take it easy and lift nothing heavier than a kettle. Lying in bed was not my forte and I felt compelled to get up and about, to do, do, do. Chris's parents stayed for a few weeks to make sure I didn't, didn't, didn't. Finally, they left and I promised not to stand on wheely chairs at the top of stairs trying to change lightbulbs or stand on the banister to readjust a wonky curtain or other such life-threatening, somewhat Autie antics.

I had recovered enough to go back to work seeing families and got busy looking for a wedding dress. The wedding was set for the ninth of December, six months after I had asked Chris and just over a year since I'd met him.

Chris chose an old college friend, Greg, to be his best man. I wanted to be liked and accepted by his friends, so I thought it might be a good idea to choose Greg's partner and long-term friend of Chris's, Cassie, to be my bridesmaid.

I found a dress pattern and went to the market with Chris, Greg and Cassie to choose some fabric for it, as well as for the bridemaid's dress and the waistcoats for Chris and Greg. Chris and I had already found patterns for the bridesmaid's dress. It was rustic and colonial, a burgundy skirt and lace-up waistcoat over a cream-coloured top. The pictures for it were honest and simple and lovely. We had a pattern for the men's waistcoats too.

Then, as we walked among the fabric stalls, hanging up on a second-hand stall was a wedding dress made of brushed silk with sequins and beads.

'Try it on,' urged Chris.

And I did. It fitted my body and it fitted with me, perfectly. I bought it.

We went on to buy the fabric for Cassie's bridesmaid's dress, a heavy embroidered burgundy for the skirt and some gold-coloured cord for the lace-up waistcoat. Then we bought the sheeny metallic embroidered satin for the men's waistcoats. Silver and black for Chris and burgundy and black for Greg.

Back in the car, Cassie asked: 'If you're not going to use that wedding dress pattern, do you mind if I use it?'

It was a literal enough question. I had no idea how she would use it and no reason to ask. I said, 'OK.'

It was a few days later when Cassie showed up at our house with something to show me and Chris. She had bought herself a white satin wedding dress. She had decided to alter it to fit the pattern I had bought for my original wedding dress and then wear it as the bridesmaid's dress.

Something in me felt suffocated. There was something wrong here but I wasn't sure what. She asked Chris what he thought of her dress as she modelled it against herself. He commented honestly that it was a nice dress.

We sat at the table and Cassie talked cynically about marriage, that there wasn't any point because if you got married you couldn't easily just change your mind. I asked why she agreed to become bridesmaid. She replied honestly that she saw it as an opportunity to dress up.

Upstairs, Cassie busied herself in helping me sort out the waistcoats for Chris and his best man Greg. She talked about my wedding dress, that if it was her she would strip the beads off and start from scratch, that after all, it wasn't really as if such a second-hand thing was really 'my' wedding dress. She quizzed me as to whether I was really sure I was doing the right thing to be getting married to her friend Chris, after all, she said, 'you've just got out of hospital', 'you don't look well', 'you hardly even know him'. I didn't know what to say and went quiet.

It was weeks later when I finally opened up to Chris about the little confidential conversations his friend had been having with me and how distressed I felt at her making herself a wedding dress for our wedding. I told Chris I would have to tell her I didn't want her as a bridesmaid.

She didn't take it well at all. Bitter emails flew in response to my request, and Cassie and Greg arranged a meeting with Chris at work. They discussed their feelings that he was making a bad decision in getting married, that it was too much of a rush, that it was too soon, that it all seemed 'too fluid' as they put it.

Chris tried to assure them that he knew what he was doing, but the atmosphere turned stony cold as Chris felt torn between the college friends of old and me. Essentially forced to choose, he chose me. Cassie returned the pattern for the wedding dress which she had already cut out and wrote saying that she would show up at the wedding in jeans so as not to offend me, and that she was only doing so because Chris needed the support. Greg continued to be best man but stopped coming around to the house.

I appointed my PA as bridesmaid and, with no time to make clothes, gave her some money to choose herself something to wear, as long as it was not a wedding dress.

The day of the wedding, we were uncertain whether Greg would show. Chris got ready alone, and Greg showed up long enough to drop off a waistcoat and tell Chris he would see him at the wedding. Chris's friend Leo showed up to usher people at the ceremony, our friend Serge arrived as our camera man, our friend Jeff showed up with his fiddle to play our music accompaniment, Al showed up ready to read poetry, and my friend Bob showed up with his partner Steve, ready to play the role of parents of the bride.

Chris emerged ready from his room in tails and white shirt, his long hair falling around him. I emerged ready from mine, flowers in my hair and small veil falling over my long curly hair. My PA emerged with me and said we both looked fabulous. Excitedly, we took hold of each other and headed for the wedding car which would take us to the registry office.

The wedding car took the long way through the trees and the forest of the hills. It gave us time for the moment to be ours, just us and nature, before it turned into the driveway of the local council building where the marriage was to take place.

Cassie awaited the car, dressed in jeans, but was swamped by Chris's parents, his brother and his fiancée, his aunt and uncle, his cousins, my hypnotherapist Natalie, one of my autie families and their teenage girl Zoe, our old next-door neighbour, two of Chris's childhood friends, a multitude of locals, and Fred and Jean from once upon a time.

Our friend started up on the fiddle as we made our way in. Exposure Anxiety had me and made it difficult to look at people, but the fiddle playing got into my legs and I danced about and clapped my hands as the service began.

Greg showed up sullen and stony and handed the ring at the right time. Cassie sat with a friend on his mobile phone who phoned up the old crowd to verify that the dreaded deed was done.

Bob stood proudly in his suit and multiple body piercings as Steve looked on.

Chris's family were moved and excited as they watched their eldest son get married.

Serge moved about in the audience getting a great video.

Finally, our audience applauded as we were pronounced married.

On the way out, I met Jean. She had barely made it here, but made it she did. As one of the few people who never triggered Exposure Anxiety in me, this very wonderfully autie woman hugged me and looked once more deeply into my eyes.

She lived two more months, then was gone.

Chris and I made our way out into the muddy gardens, as people crowded together for makeshift photos. I forgot myself and poked out my tongue trying to look at the camera, then looking away so that I might be able to look back long enough for the shot. Then the car whisked us away to a place called Cottage In The Woods where we had our bridal suite. Our honeymoon proper was in one week's time. I would take Chris off to visit my own country. We would make a pilgrimage back to Australia.

We boarded the plane for Australia and arrived in Bali on the way. I had been well since the operation and treated myself to a pineapple and coconut juice as we sat in the open air in this tropical paradise country.

We caught a taxi out to the monkey forest and watched monkeys throwing themselves into a pond, dive-bombing each other and jumping back out to run away. We watched them play rhythms with rocks they had found, rolling them to smooth their surfaces before trying the sound again.

We went to dances with drumming and cymbals, masks and dragons, hands moving like music as dancers moved in a flurry around the night-time stage within this outdoor temple.

We went to a sacred temple where fruit and rice were left for the Hindu gods and the streets were lined with people asking 'Transport?', 'You need transport?'

Next stop Melbourne, with its trams and cosmopolitan city atmosphere. We arrived at our holiday house and set up a temporary Christmas tree in this country where Santa dressed in warm winter reds during the beachside barbecue season.

Cockatoos and rosella parrots landed on our front veranda to eat seed. Chris had never seen such large or colourful birds beyond a book or TV screen. At night a possum came up to the back door; Chris wondered what this boggle-eyed furry thing was, and we threw it bread.

We went up to the reservoir where three wedge-tailed eagles circled above us, the underneath of their wings decorated in deep brown and ochre patterns that looked like eyes peering down. We passed a field of lazing kangaroos.

Down the coast we visited the massive sandstone structures of the Twelve Apostles, a few of which had since collapsed under the strain of the ocean. We watched the waves crash ferociously, throwing tall showers of foam high into the air as they hit the pillars which had dared to live out from the shore. I drew cartoons in the sand and danced barefoot on the gold grainy surface. We explored a beachside cave and climbed over sandstone structures sculpted by the wind and the ocean.

We rode trams through the city at night, the trees lit up with strings of lights, and walked through the city gardens visiting the fairy tree.

We invited a few of my friends around to the holiday house and showed them the wedding video. They liked Chris, and he liked them.

It felt strange being here without my father. So we visited his grave. It was in a dusty dry bush cemetery with golden clay earth and not a flower in sight. We stood at the foot of the grave, and I introduced Chris to my father.

It was time to go home back to the UK. On the way, I asked Chris what he thought of Australia. I asked if he would ever like to live there. He had loved it and yes, he would think about living there.

Back in the UK, Serge was glad to see us. As I visited his office in the old antiques store, I saw a series of used canvases. I asked him about them and he said he could get them for me for a good price. They were large, really large, with the biggest one of them about five-foot high by six-foot wide. I bought them. All I would have to do was begin painting.

A van delivered the canvases, and Chris came down the shops with me to make it a reality that I had the paints to paint with. We bought a load of oil paints and brushes and went home.

With Exposure Anxiety it is all or nothing. Either something sits there all year or it gets done straight away. The canvases stared at me, putting me under pressure. Then they shouted to the world to look at how I had done nothing to them. I defied them and began to paint. Then they would be silenced.

I went to work on the biggest canvas and turned it around and around till an image began to jump out at me from the mess. I worked with the image, bringing it out, letting it speak to me. A boy emerged. It was a boy I had worked in consultancy with, a young boy named Oliver. The look was expectant yet full of trepidation. The colours were explosive like a Van Gogh. I called it 'Next' and hung it on the wall.

Serge came over to view it and was gob-smacked. He just stood there with his hand over his mouth shaking his head. Then he threw his hand out to the side as though in disbelief. 'This is brilliant, Donna,' he spluttered. 'Really, this is … amazing.'

After that, everyone who saw it seemed awestruck. It was like I had taken all my artistic ability, stored it up and, like with *Nobody Nowhere* and with my sculpture 'My World–The World', or as with my CD, I had concentrated it all into this first painting. I felt certain it couldn't be that I could really paint that well. I painted another canvas, then another, then another, again and again, each remarkably different from the last, but each of equal ability. The paintings were engaging. They brought out an empathy like looking at one's soul in a reflection. I couldn't help feeling that these abilities came from somewhere else, that there was more than just me speaking through my hands to the typewriter, to the clay, to the piano, to the canvas. It was like all with whom I had resonated had enriched my preconscious reality and that given the right trigger it would come through. For me, the boundaries of who was in which body weren't as concrete as our conceptualization would have us imagine. In the reality of sensing and resonance, this simply wasn't so. The living were not merely within their own bodies, the dead were never really gone. We were somehow part of every person who had ever moved us or who had been a catalyst for change, and they were part of us, if we, in our rigid ideas of self, so allowed it to be.

Chris set about getting papers for migration to Australia. It was real. After twelve years away, I was really going back. I couldn't believe it. But instead of feeling ecstatic, I began to be gripped with dread, and I began to get sick again.

It was one cold after another, every six weeks another bug and they would hang on like it was going to be them or me, and they were certain it was going to be them.

I got angry with my body and felt compelled to starve it. Then I became afraid this would make me sicker, so I disclosed to Chris what I was getting caught up in. I explained that I was angry at my body for letting me get sick again, that I had fallen out with it, and that I would starve it till it behaved itself.

Chris explained that my body didn't mean to make me sick, that it was sick and it needed my help.

I raged back at him, retorting that I had been doing my best and my body knew it. I had given it all the supplements it needed to stay healthy. I had kept my body warm. I gave it exercise. Why was it so angry with me? I hit myself in the face unable to contain the rage.

Chris took my hand and stroked my face saying 'poor face'. Then he took some objects and used them to explain how my body couldn't hear me and it wasn't out to get me. He explained that my body didn't want the viruses but that it couldn't fight them. He suggested I could go back to Dr Kenyon. I wanted a real solution. I was sick of these health breakdowns. The slightest sign of stress and it all went kaput. So what, I had a myalgic condition that caused inflammation throughout my body whenever I got stressed. I wanted it gone. I wanted a properly functioning immune system.

I went to the GP who did another blood test. The transfer factor from Dr Kenyon had done its job. For the first time I got a normal white cell count. So what was wrong?

I sent off a urine sample for analysis to a pharmacologist called Paul Shattock at Sunderland University. I knew I was dairy-intolerant and used to have an allergy to wheat, but Dr Kenyon said I was over my allergy to wheat and showed no sign of gluten allergy. It was one shred of hope. Perhaps this was the problem.

The urine analysis came back. It showed undigested proteins, which clearly fit the profile of gluten intolerance that Paul Shattock had found in eighty per cent of people with autism. I asked how this could be when I was not allergic to gluten. Paul explained that you can have the gluten intolerance with or without developing the allergy.

So I was now off gluten, and for three days I went through a severe withdrawal. I paced and I raged and I bit and slapped my face and cried in frustration as my emotional state went even more chaotic. Then the fog cleared and stayed clear as the days progressed. But still the viruses clung to me.

Then I heard of another clinic which treated immune deficiency. It was run by a naturopath and biochemist called Mike Ash. I had a saliva test for secretory IgA, a shorthand for immunoglobulin A, the immunity of the mucous membranes of the ears, nose, throat, lungs and gut, and the body's first line of defence. IgA is the messenger that tells your white cells what bugs you've got. It's effectively the brains behind the activity of white cells. No IgA, no IgG or immunoglobulin G. No IgG, no cell memory for what you've caught either. So first of all, you can't recognize it in order to take the action to fight it; and secondly, even if you somehow get that far then you have no cell memory to stop you from catching it again and again. So people with no Secretory IgA could, for example, catch something like the measles more than once and lack the gut immune response to properly recognize and respond to vaccinations. Secretory IgA would do more than this. Without this IgA the body would not recognize proteins properly and wouldn't give the signal to send the right enzymes for digestion. It was beginning to make sense.

Normal levels of Secretory IgA fell between 93 and 290. Anything below 60 is considered a deficiency. Mine was 13 and considered to be essentially none at all. So finally I had my answer. I fell into the twenty per cent of people with autism who had an IgA deficiency and of those the eight per cent who had no IgA at all. Even more shocking, many children with this deficiency go undiagnosed, receiving, like I had, year after year of antibiotics till their health simply collapses. Because most doctors, even immunologists, are not naturopaths as well, even those diagnosed can go without any kind of introduction to the treatments that might change their immune status.

Mike Ash explained that with that count I was lucky to have made it as far as I had and that this was why I simply carried viruses which would die back down only to flare up later, that essentially I probably hadn't fought them off at all. Then came the good news. Mike had a programme designed to boost secretory IgA within six weeks. It involved taking, among other things, massive doses of an immune boosting supplement which tasted like hell and, even worse, contained traces of oat bran, soya and hydrolysed whey protein. Was he mad? I'd be off my rocker. He explained that these were only fillers in the product and that the high doses of immune boosters would so raise my immune status that the gut problems and allergy responses would not be seen. I was very scared but I trusted him, and he was right. Finally, he also suggested eating earthworms.

I thought this guy was off his rocker. Eating earthworms? But apparently, these particular earthworms could trick my body into believing it had parasites so it would switch from an inflammatory and allergic state into one where it would go to war with the army of bugs which had taken up permanent residence in me. The earthworms were powdered and in capsules. I took them together with the immune boosting mud-like stuff. Six weeks later, I was retested. To our delight my IgA count was now a healthy 192 – smack in the middle of the normal range and not a bug in sight.

'Great,' I said. 'So what's the plan now? How long am I on this stuff?'

Mike explained that some people only have a mild deficiency and you can pick them up a bit and send them on their way and their system can repair itself. In my case, the good news was that this help existed. The bad news was that if I wanted to stay healthy, I would have to stay on the programme for the rest of my life.

I had a few children on my books who appeared to have immune deficiency. I gave their families a call and told them about the IgA test. All of them tested under 60; the lowest of their scores was 20.

Like all good rebels, I had to test the water. I dabbled in gluten and got a thick head, but otherwise no problem. I came off it and, sure enough, on day three it was as though I'd taken bitch pills. I was going through withdrawal. I decided that I had enough problems trying to think straight and keep emotional stability without this crap. If every time the levels of this protein in my blood began to decrease I would go through a junkie's withdrawal, I didn't need bread that badly. I set about discovering all the gluten-free dairy-free breads, crackers, cakes, pancake mixes, biscuits, puddings, pizza bases and gravy I could find, and ended up with a more varied diet than before.

I felt so well I decided I was now cured of my immune deficiency and came off the supplements. I lasted two weeks before a bug got me again. I decided to behave myself.

Chris's migration papers had come back in the post. He had got past the preliminary hurdles. Now a health check, a police check, letters about our relationship. We were going. We were really going. Yet I knew deep in my heart that coping with stress was going to be essential to beating immune deficiency and gut problems. There were some things I hadn't faced up to. I went back to Natalie for hypnotherapy.

I explained to her that there was something I hadn't told anyone, something which ate at me and for which I couldn't forgive myself.

I told her about the animals I had brought home and what had happened to them. I explained how I then stirred the gravy which I believed helped poison my own father. I had already seen what had happened to the dog and still did nothing, nothing to stop it. I had been unable to communicate directly and personally in those days and there was nobody who could have helped me. But even in the years that followed, I told her, as I fought to open up and join the world, I sought only to save myself. I ran and kept running and didn't look back. I left everyone to fight for themselves. Now there would be no 'sorry'.

I was in pieces. I felt crushed like I could barely breathe. I feared the whole world would detest me, that all the esteem with which it had ever held me up would suddenly be seen as a waste of breath spent on a wretched and dirtied little girl. I had proclaimed to the world that my background compelled me to escape the confines of my 'autism' and inspired me how to do it. But my background had also left me with post-traumatic stress disorder, which most never got close enough to see, a stress disorder that undermined my health, which in turn exacerbated my 'autism'.

'You were just a child, Donna,' said Natalie. 'Do you hear me? You had one obligation, only one, to survive. Nobody will hold that against you. Even your father would have understood. If he were here now, he wouldn't hold it against you. You didn't kill your father. He died of cancer. It may have come sooner because of what happened, but you didn't have a choice. He'd understand that.'

I couldn't believe that I had heard that out loud in my own ears, heard those events spoken out loud in the world. It had begun with a poem, and from writing, it was finally told in words out loud in the world. Now I knew that if I went back to the country from which I had been in self-imposed exile, that I would go back in openness and honesty, afraid of no skeletons in the closet and clear, very very clear, that with the death of my father, my relationship to that family was finally at an end. I was a child of the world. I was Chris's family, and he and his family were mine.

I wished so badly that I knew who my father's confidante had been, the woman he had written of, who listened to him in the midst of the war we both lived in all those years ago.

I remembered a lady who used to visit our house. Her name was Christine. She had done so for years and had known me from the age of seven right up till I was ten when the war was so horribly bad. Her husband had been Jackie Paper's best friend, then he died in a trucking accident along with her only daughter, a gentle honest simple girl just two years younger than me. Christine had disappeared just after that.

I went on the internet and did a search for her surname in the area she had lived in all those years ago. Only one entry came up with the name. I called it.

'Hello,' I said. 'I used to be called Donna Williams; my father knew a lady with the surname Mamoud.'

It turned out the number belonged to this woman's mother-in-law and, yes, she had the number for her.

I called Christine. Her voice hadn't changed from the bubbly, down-to-earth giggler she had been as a visitor to the house all those years ago.

She started crying. She said she remembered how I was treated and had always worried and wondered what had happened to me. She was so surprised to hear me speaking, for in all the two hundred or so times she had visited our house when I was growing up, she only ever heard me mutter to myself. In her experience, I never spoke.

I asked her about my father, and she replied: 'Of course I knew him, him and me were great mates. He used to sneak over here at least once a week. We weren't sleeping together, nothing like that. He helped me take care of my boy after his father and sister were killed. He was fabulous with him, used to throw him up onto his shoulders, give him shoulder rides, tickle him and chase him through the house. He was exactly what he needed. He made him laugh.'

She told me how she heard he had died and said how much she missed him. I asked if she had seen him often in the years before his death. She said he visited with them for about ten years and that he would come around and let off steam about what was going on in the house and all the things he couldn't change.

'You know he loved you,' she said.

'Yeah', I replied. 'I do.'

I had found my father's confidante.

I had six months of tremendous health before a flu virus wiped me out. It was the longest period of time without bugs that I could remember in years. And the virus stayed, four weeks, then six weeks, then nine weeks. The behavioural tics were back: involuntary breath holding; the constant muscle tensing which clicked the muscles of my inner ears and left my neck and shoulders so stressed and tight that I constantly cricked my neck; face slapping and biting. These had changed constantly over the years from spitting to throat clearing, to sudden arm movements and phrase repetitions. They always seemed to flare up when I had bugs. On top of this, the Exposure Anxiety made it impossible to stay seated when I wanted to be, and had me struggling with eating, drinking, the toilet and getting a jumper. I wanted to be on my body's side, but these crazy impulses were counting against me.

I took my immune boosters but they did no good. I even took them in double dose as my hands began to turn orange from an overdose of vitamin A. I called Dr Danczak, a collegue of Dr Kenyon's who ran an international newsletter about autism management. He talked me out of a panic and convinced me that the bug I had really needed some antibiotics in spite of my well-founded fear of them.

Then in my desperate search of the internet for a solution to the tics that were causing me such distress, I came across a medication. It was called Risperidone and had been given in dosages as small as 0.5mgs to stop behavioural tics, and for Obsessive Compulsive Disorder (OCD), Bipolar (Manic Depression) and Panic Disorder. It had once been a drug reserved in large doses for Schizophrenia but had recently become one of the most successful drugs used for involuntary and self-injurious behaviours in people with autism. I phoned a psychiatrist I knew of called Steven Hinder and asked him about it. Yes, he had run a trial with forty people with autism who had involuntary and self-injurious behaviours, and thirty-eight of them lost their involuntary behaviours on this small dose. He spoke of Reward Deficiency Syndrome, essentially a condition in which people became addicted to their own adrenaline and which affected people as diverse as compulsive gamblers through to alcoholics, people with OCD and ADHD (a percentage of whom are misdiagnosed cases of Rapid Cycling Childhood Bipolar Disorder) among others.

I knew that the higher I buzzed in manic oblivion, the more I was simultaneously feeding the grip of self-protection responses which would get me around the next corner. Both were governed by adrenaline responses gone mad. I understood the cycle of chronic anxiety suppressing immunity, impairing digestion and messing up the supply of nutrients to the brain and the neurotransmitters responsible for behaviour. I could remember emotional fits, incredible euphoric highs and overwhelming self-directed rages before the age of four, which happened at least six times a day. Diet and supplementation in adulthood had certainly turned down the volume, allowing me to suppress most of it when in public, but it didn't take it away, and this wasn't a psychological problem I could undermine with hypnotherapy.

There are many addicts who really don't want their drug any more, but one brief taste of it and they are hooked again. It was the prison warder sitting back waiting for the slightest sign to justify its right to 'protect' me. I had learned to sing and give myself a rhythm to make it unaware, to convince myself I was indifferent about all I wanted so it wouldn't block me from taking actions, to find ways to act as something or someone else, for anyone other than myself or hide within the company of my safe person so it wouldn't interfere with my expression. I had found strategies to hold meaning when it cut me off from connection to my own words or those coming in, and had found ways to trigger emotional response when it refused to let them be shared with the world. I could do all of this, but I could not undo the addiction itself. It was simple, this addiction to adrenaline, which I'd likely inherited from two rather biloar parents, made my body respond like a glutton. A small amount of stress would be focused on till it was enormous.

But the thing that jumped out at me most about the write-up on this medication was that it was used to treat what was termed 'Panic Disorder'. Though this was not specifically Exposure Anxiety, what if, just what if, the tics, OCD, Bipolar Disorder and Exposure Anxiety were actually all related. What if this medication took away the invisible cage of self-protection mechanisms? Think of the energy I'd have back if I wasn't fighting and suppressing these impulses all day, every day of my life. Was it possible that, if this took away the Exposure Anxiety, I wouldn't suffer from immune deficiency?

I made an appointment with the GP. He had sent off a sample of my coughed up green chest 'muck' nine weeks ago. Now I sat here, still riddled with a lung virus I couldn't fight and asking for antipsychotics. He knew I had autism, and he himself had a daughter who was high-functioning and on the spectrum. Still, he wondered how I thought this atypical antipsychotic would help me. I explained my theory. I explained the problems I had with tics and how these always got worse when I was sick with a bug. I explained the impact of OCD traits on driving Chris mad by going on and on about a topic which was stressing me, day in day out, sometimes for months on end no matter how desperately I myself was sick of obsessing, though I failed to tell him of the manic giggling fits and euphoria I would later come to look upon as Rapid Cycling Childhood Bipolar Disorder. Then I went into a whisper, explaining gently, almost so I myself couldn't hear, that there was something else. I explained that I had wished all my life for just one day without the challenges of Exposure Anxiety, one day of just getting a drink whenever I wanted, being able to grab a coat without a struggle, able to stay sitting among friends instead of compelled to constantly leave the room, to be able to eat regularly without retaliation. 'Most importantly,' I said starting to cry, 'I don't even know the luxury of taking a pee when I need one.'

He explained that this drug had side-effects, but conceded that in my thin state the weight gain wouldn't hurt and that the dosage of 0.5mgs was so small it was less likely to do much long-term harm. He prescribed me a thirty-day supply.

I took a tablet as soon as the pharmacist handed them over. Then I headed home.

My friend Bob dropped around about two hours later. He was just passing by. I listened to him from the other side of the table and thought it strange that I was so mellow, no ants in my pants. He said something which moved me and I asked, to my own surprise, if I could give him a hug. He nearly fell off his chair. He had known me for four years, and though I could cringingly tolerate a hug I was far from able to initiate hugs with my friends.

'Sure,' he spluttered, with a look of 'Um, how should I help you with this'.

I hugged my friend and it felt free and freeing. It moved me, everything seemed to move me. I had lost my fleas. I had no monkey on my back. I was seeing who was underneath all of that. Finally, all I had ever wished to know was in my hands, but instead of only getting it for that one day I had wished for all my life, I had been handed it for thirty.

Chris phoned up and I was chirpy on the phone, looking forward to him coming home. Waiting for him, I needed a pee and simply went, catching myself just walking straight in there like an escapee waiting for the prison warder who was nowhere in sight. I sat on the loo and cried. I couldn't believe it. Thirty-eight years old and finally it was that easy.

Chris came home and I looked straight at him, none of the involuntary diverting from his gaze in the expectation he would be looking to connect. For over a year we had played 'autie eyes', him avoiding my eye contact in order to play hard to get and thereby provoke me to compete to get him to look at me. In the yes equals no and no equals yes reality of Exposure Anxiety it always worked.

'We won't need autie eyes any more from the look of it,' said Chris smiling.

I warmed into the feel of his body and started crying, bragging about how easy it was to go to the loo and offering to make him a cup of tea. That night I didn't just make him one cup of tea, I made him six. I got stuck into the cupboard and put together a meal with no diversions. It was like my once fragmented thought processes were sticky-taped together, and my actions flowed like a well-played classic. That night he got into bed and I was far from in my own world. I sat propped up on my elbow looking at him with such directness. He responded with shyness.

At the end of the thirty days I had hugged Chris's parents, eaten regularly, initiated going out, easily stayed sitting with my friends and visitors, enjoyed the privilege of grabbing a jumper when I needed one, got a drink whenever I felt like it and had come to enjoy the toilet like a good movie. The only fear I had was that the doctor might not re-prescribe the medication. It wasn't a problem.

In the months that followed, I celebrated freedom from tics and obsession and extreme mood swings, and the freedom to express and act upon a want, but I got something else too. Within four weeks of being on the medication, the chest infection that had plagued me for nine weeks had cleared up. I thought it was a fluke. At the same time, I had had to come off the immune boosters because their vitamin A content was causing liver problems. But instead of getting sick again, I stayed well.

C hris's papers had come through. It was official. He was granted Australian residency. I was going home.

I would so miss my friends, Serge and Bob, Rosita and my old neighbour Merril. I would miss my in-laws, whom I had only just begun to hug of my own volition and who had so openly welcomed this strange misfit of a daughter-in-law. I would miss Britain as my adopted home of twelve years and Natalie who had so helped me adjust to such change and loss and celebration.

We boarded the plane on 24th September 2002, one week after sending off the final draft of my latest textbook, *Exposure Anxiety: The Invisible Cage.* We were uncertain as to exactly where we would end up, just that we were committed to the adventure. Fritz was right all those years ago when he picked me up as a hitchhiker – I was a travelling girl.

I awoke one morning with a big snuggly hairy man curled into the shape of my back snoring gently. I had sent out my CDs to local radio stations a few weeks before and wondered, just wondered. I reached over to the clock radio next to my side of the bed and flicked the switch to radio. My voice came out of the speakers singing back at me one of the songs from my album called *Just A Little Bit of Time.* I sang along with it laughing as Chris woke up…

*Just a little bit of time is maybe all it takes to face this journey I've been making,*
*All the chances never taken.*
*Just a little bit of time is maybe all I need to cross this line without me losing,*
*All the fight it took in choosing.*
*Just a little bit of time could be the net to catch me falling,*
*And just a little bit of time could be the place I hear you calling, me.*
*Calling me.*

Lightning Source UK Ltd.
Milton Keynes UK
UKOW04f2317130914

238469UK00004B/165/P